LIFE'S

STOP

LIGHTS

RED EDITION: WHAT'S STOPPING YOU?

M.L. Smiley McGinnis

Dedicated to my loving wife and our three children. For all the time that was lost in the busyness of work and not in my life's work. And the unforgiveable disappointments and hurt by not being fully present. For this, I can only be sorry once more. Moving forward, we have so much more to generate, enjoy and love.

With an infinitude of gratitude and love,

Smiley/Dad

Written for those who refuse to allow limiting beliefs, mediocrity, and complacency to dictate anything less than your highest self.

"Anyone or anything that is not contributing to your highest self is too small for you."

LIFE'S STOP LIGHTS

10 CHAPTERS TO GREEN LIGHT THE TRUEST YOU

Introduction

I am both honored and grateful that you have purchased my book. I am eager to bring forth, uncover and allow you to fully understand what is holding you back begetting your biggest rival – and to be transparently honest, **You**. It is often stated that "You are your biggest and harshest critic." Why? Society and most people reinforce it by being cruel, limited thinkers. However, the time is now to break the yoke that you did not know you were carrying; to start living for whom you were made, not what everyone else thinks who you should or will be in the future. It is time to be genuine and explicit with yourself and those you encounter over your lifetime. By not living and doing what you were made for is like slapping the face of your Maker.

After you learn about limiting beliefs, it is sobering how these false beliefs have and continue to shape not only you, but societies and the world. You all have limiting beliefs, it is a matter of mining, studying and reprogramming these disempowering and limiting beliefs into core strengths and becoming who you are meant to be, now and forever remembered.

I know that you will find what is written to be telling, eye opening and will generate some internal, deep thinking and discussions, *provided you* are *completely honest with yourself and keeping an open heart and mind*. Take this book earnestly, as a tool, to help you become an e-ven better version of yourself today and to become the highest version of yourself before leaving your decisive legacy.

Fear is controlling everyone today. Fear has a strangle hold on each one of us. Fear is sucking the courage right out of you. You have become afraid of everything that you do, think, act, post and dream. Fear causes you to stand apart, to stand indifferently, to stand and live in fear. We hold a fear in everything from hurting feelings to familial drama to terrorism to even a nuclear war. The vastness is a little drastic, but I hope it makes you think, clearly and honorably.

This fear that controls us, began as a limiting belief seed, planted within us at some point. You have cultivated and reassured it through acceptance and without question, allowing this seedling to root, grow, branch and to take control in all areas of your life, like a noxious weed.

The time is NOW to pull this "limiting belief weed" to start fresh and anew.

Throughout your journey of discovery, you will be participating with written activities to decide, identify and then begin to remove disempowering or limiting beliefs from within you and even your loved ones, both close and afar. You will learn a technique to generate an alternative solution and lastly, challenging you to have the self-discipline to follow through with your new habits and responses. Life is not only about choices, but knowing that you made a difference beyond yourself, having loved reciprocally and unconditionally, and lived a life fully and free of fears. My hope is that you will join this inspiring movement to eliminate limited and negative thinking, empower choice and engage conscious minds around the world to create a lasting and affirmative legacy, far reaching beyond your years touching seven generations from now.

You must open your eyes and heart and be explicitly honest as to where we are headed as a world. You have become complacent by not asking, "Why?" Truth be told, it is this simple. It may sound like common sense, but it has not been common practice.

As a child, we practiced the insistent questioning of absolutely everything. Why do I need to _____? Why do I have to _____? Why should I ___? **Why? Why? Why? Why?**

As a teenager, you had questions but now with a little more depth and knowledge. You question things grounded on where and how you were raised and by whom, directly or indirectly and how they had imparted their beliefs in you.

Why do I need to complete high school? Why do I need to spend over $100,000 to receive a piece of paper (Degree) that supposedly makes me better than 90% of the world? Why can't I go out on a school night? **Why? Why? Why?**

Then as an adult, you have gone from the feeling of having great skills, knowledge and communications but yet, unknowingly become timid, tender and conditioned not to ask. Why do you have to sit at a red light when there isn't a hint of another vehicle anywhere close to you? When did a light bulb become smarter than you? Why don't we have a better public and affordable transportation system, *Nationwide*? Why do you continue to rely on fossil fuels? Why do you have to be, at least in the United States, bombarded with "commercials of testimonials and claims", which you know are not true or even possible? **Why? Why?**

And finally, you reach your golden years and are nearing the end of your ride on this big ball we call Earth. Why didn't I spend more time with my family? Why did I work so much and play so little? Why didn't I love more openly and often? Why did I let money decide if I was successful? Why do we allow an individual, who lacks morals, values and similar beliefs, to make decisions on your behalf? **Why?**

You must start asking more difficult and purposeful questions. You can read about anything and everything and do this using only your fingertips. Moreover, society is starving from the lack of wisdom in our lives. We have all this information, more than one can read, about all subjects, but are missing how to apply them in your life. Then, why do you have to follow unwritten societal rules when you have so much more potential and opportunity, literally at your fingertips? Why do you need to continue being just a sheep in a worldly flock, fearing wolves? Why will you not push yourself harder to reach greater aspirations? Why can't you have everything that you want? What is stopping you in accomplishing and doing more? Why is (_?_) holding you back from more? Who is holding you back?

You.

Live fully with embodiment and acceptance of your inner "go light" and rejecting your "caution or stop lights." The time is NOW, to break down your life's stop lights, follow your heart, chase your dreams and create a healthier world, starting with you and again, now.

Seek answers. Who had the most influence in your life and career? What did they do to have so much influence within you? Who influences you now? Bottom line, we all need a "coach". You are becoming more complacent, comfortable and less of a critique of entitlements and fairness. The universe rewards action.

"The World offers you comfort, but you were not made for comfort. You were made for greatness." -Pope Benedict XVI

Life's Stop Lights, a 3 Book Sequence:
Red, Yellow and Green

Congratulations on taking the first steps towards finding and re-introducing the authentic **you**. This book series is written for you and anyone else who has lost themselves in *busy work*, and not your *life's work*. I am honored and enthusiastic that you too, will take this journey of self-discovery towards becoming who **you** were designed. Decide. Discover. Embrace.

With the upmost transparency and honesty, I do want to forewarn you, as the journey you are about to embark, is not an easy one, nor one to be taken **light**ly. You will be dealing with feelings, emotions, conditions, and challenging long standing beliefs that may have anchored, unknowingly within yourself. To help in the process of identification, change, habits and growth, I have broken this *journey of self-discovery* into 3 sequential books.

Each edition will build even more self-awareness, self-discovery. During the book series, you will come to realize a crowning point, a point of direction that you have not had in the past. You will be even more capable and willing to jolt others into bold action by coaching and sharing what you have learned, applied and succeeded throughout your journey of self-discovery with everyone life brings to you. You will be emotionally committed in helping others seek their true giving purpose and self. You will uncover cognitive distortions of which you may or may not be aware, and how to deal with these too. Again, it will not be stress-free, but liberating.

Book One: <u>Life's Stop Lights</u> _ Red Edition, What's stopping You? is where you decide, identify and begin to act on your limiting beliefs, authenticity of self, congruency, cognitive dissonance and distortions, mediocrity and minimalism, developing a quiet mind, finding clarity and consistency and learning from this Author's life challenges that are not necessarily unique.

You will be able to detect how you are subconsciously *limiti*ng yourself. The core purpose is to be able to decide, detect or identify and act on *your limiting beliefs* that are holding you back from living a free and fulfilling life.

Book Two: <u>Life's Stop Lights</u> -Yellow Edition, What's your Why? is where we continue peeling back the layers of hidden and disempowering beliefs, self-sabotaging events and cognitive distortions. All the while, honing our abilities and sharpening our tools to be able to create a command goal or a "cautioning" phrase to use when we feel ourselves swaying back into our old, bad habits and planting disempowering limits. The core purpose is to be able to identify not only in you, but within others, what is holding us back from reaching our given purpose and greatness.

Book Three: <u>Life's Stop Lights</u> – Who will you help? is where you begin to further refine your skills, knowledge and abilities. Building fortifications, buzz words or phrases to stop yourself from limited thinking and negative self-talk in all areas of your life. Utilizing growth representations to ensure continued success, growth and coaching; all while *you* live more vibrantly, confidently and mindfully. The core purpose of this book is to feel comfortable in asking "why?" with no resentment, regrets and disempowerments standing in your way.

Throughout all three books, challenges, examples and exercises will allow you to think, learn and grow yourself out of negative self-talk and disempowering and limited beliefs. Please complete these exercises as the Universe rewards Action. You absolutely need to be brutally honest and transparent with yourself during these exercises. No more excuses, reasons, answers, or self-justifications. Take bold action. Own your destiny. Own your choices. Own your life again.

These "exercises and challenges" can and are encouraged to be shared with family, friends, colleagues, and even people you meet along your journey of self-discovery.

Caution: Shelf Knowledge: To know and not do is not yet to know.

In other words, don't just read the book (*to know*) and *not do* the exercises or practice the principles; you cannot wish or think yourself to a goal to not yet to know.

Foreword

How many of us, I wonder, can recall a childhood moment when we experienced happiness as a state of presence – that *simple moment of untarnished joyfulness* – that moment when everything in our World, inside and out, was unspoiled?

Soberly, we have become a collection of adults where everything is wrong – all the time – on a quest to get it back. We truthfully experience happiness as a by-product, a side effect. Happiness is found and enjoyed in your pursuit along with gratitude. It really is in the thrill of the chase. Remember when you were (are) vying for a date with that special someone? The novelty and challenge of getting that first date …that is pure happiness. Relive it. Believe it. Achieve it.

93%! 93% of people are not living a fulfilled or happy life. 7% are, well, in that *simple moment of untarnished joyfulness*, infinitely. What is the secret to live like the 7%? Read on……

My giving-purpose in researching self-sabotaging beliefs, cognitive dissonance and distortions is to help people. I will continue to be a _student of excellence_; to continue mastery on human performance, conversion, clarity and transpersonal growth. Accomplishing this by strengthening, polishing, and creating inventive realizations. By defining, identifying, generating and sharing via easily adaptable and implementable pieces, methods and habit-breaking ways in dealing with your disempowering or limiting beliefs. This is how you will re-train yourself to live like the 7%.

This movement is far greater than improving existing lives; it is about making a difference with those who **will** exist, perform, negotiate and respect their environments 7 plus generations from now. Plant the fact-seed and watch it grow within your life and through others.

I honestly believe that you too were made for greatness too. Don't live life as it is; but as it could be. Believe in yourself and all of those that surround you. If so, you will live a life feeling more fulfilled, loved and with sincerest gratitude and appreciation for all the beautiful things in your life. Stop polarizing, generalizing and disqualifying the negatives in your past and present life. How do we find these "untarnished moments of joyfulness"? Where can you turn? Who can you ask? Why are we not taught this at home or in schools? We find all of our answers within the pursuit of our goals and yourself. Socrates said, "Learning is about remembering."

Therefore, *honesty* and *clarity* are vitally important in defining your new-found identity. Without honesty, clarity and discipline, there can be no true happiness. Maybe you are wearing a façade of *being happy*, but really you are not so. Quit. Be You. Life is precious, you owe it to yourself and others to be who you were created to be, now.

I applaud everyone whether it was a life changing event or conscious choice to live more productively, graciously and respectfully that they have just "received" a second chance in life. While you accept your second chance at life, beyond starting anew, fresh and vibrantly, you grow to feel an obligation. An obligation and gut-feeling that you must share your experience story, lessons, love for life and consciously following your destiny, ultimately generating your legacy. All the wiser that life is justly precious.

I put pen to paper to enlighten those of you who subconsciously generate disempowering, concerning, unworthy circumstances (assumptions) that instantaneously incite fear, panic, alarm and regret or limit yourself and others. I know that by applying the techniques and lessons shared thus far, with far more to follow, you will learn to slow time, control your thoughts and practice centeredness or being on task all the time.

As I was led to *believe* and have since verified through inner-viewing (and still do) hundreds of people of all ages, I could solidify this simple belief: "Nobody lies on their death bed, wishing that they had just one more day to work." No matter where inner-view-ees were in their life or career, many admittedly agreed they don't even lie in bed, alive and well, and get excited to go to work. What kind of life is this to lead? However, if you are amongst the 7%, living your dreams, feeling completely fulfilled and enjoying the precious moments of perpetual and untarnished joyfulness, you can use this book series to learn new skills, coach me and others and to further develop the impact of your legacy.

Too many people were not living as they had wanted and unfortunately, even more died with their life's spirit, core genius or Gifts, still inside, for one hundred *good* excuses and answers but no respectable reason. Maybe they died too young, had fears, lacked courage. Or maybe they were not comfortable sharing their passion, goals, dreams and Gifts. Have you explored and discovered your true meaning and giving purpose? Have you sat in the classroom of silence and listened for what God or the universe has planned for you? Have you shared with others your dreams, aspirations, memories and moments of untarnished joyfulness? Are you living in complete **congruency**? Honestly? Consistently? Do so. Do it now. You deserve it.

So many of us have accepted these beliefs as fact and have diverted our given purpose driven life away from our core genius or desire. By the time, you complete *Life's Stop Lights* series, you too, will be able to *coach* others to question their actions based on disempowering and limiting beliefs and cognitive distortions. You will ignite the fire in the bellies of millions, joining a powerful, positive and productive movement. You will be amongst the elite of the elite. The best of the best. For you will be your best, highest version of yourself.

My purpose in writing these books is simple. I have lived (and still do, too often) in fear, with disempowering and limiting beliefs controlling so many areas and aspects of my life. Despite deciding, identifying and being actively coached, I continue to consciously battle these dream killers, internally and externally. Like you, I too am a student of excellence, fully dedicated and devoted.

I am committed to humanizing, creating and sharing my Gifts by helping others. No matter your situation, you are not alone in having something holding you back or diverted from pure and untarnished joyfulness.

However, if you awake, excited to get to "work" then this book will be a quick, good refreshing read. For the rest of us (93%), this book series will serve as a recipe for changing your life to live like the 7%. Learning is truly remembering. Remembering how life once was for you too, before you established disempowering, limiting beliefs and cognitive distortions. You are not alone.

Again, **93% of you are not genuinely happy**. Whether it is your financial, educational, recreational, health/physical/psychological, relational, professional/ personal, spiritual or in your contribution to the world life areas, there is something that is not congruent within you, creating a disconnect or cognitive dissonance. It is believed, by many scholars, spiritual leaders, coaches and myself that we are born with a "*spirit, giving-purpose* or *core genius.*"

Have you ever been told that you are ornery, witty, smart, brilliant, beautiful, mysterious not functioning at your highest ability? How do some people pick up on this vibe or aura, while others do not? Why does it inspire some and scares others? Could it be that you allow yourself to meet only so many people, or let so many of them, openly into your life, keeping to yourself, afraid of being hurt, embarrassed, characterized or like I was after a horrific accident, categorized and labeled?

I am not anyone special, just another human being that is fixated on helping beyond myself. An average person who had a "dysfunctional" childhood, growing up with an alcoholic father, workaholic and dedicated mother, 6 brothers, no sisters and competition was (is) fierce. Jack Canfield said in a workshop that 85% of families in the United States are "dysfunctional." So, armed with this "new" information, no more excuses, reasons, answers or self-justifications moving forward, okay? Honesty. Integrity. Genuineness. Authenticity. Nothing less.

Quoting the late Steve Jobs, "It comes from saying "No" to 1,000 things to make sure we don't get on the wrong track or try to do too much. We're always thinking about new markets we could enter, but it's only by saying "No" that you can concentrate on the things that are really important."

In my professional life, I reached a point where I wasn't happy with my career path – as it was rewarded and filled with mediocrity, complacency and minimalism which drove me nuts. So, I tried making a change. I thought that I had a good head on my shoulders, strong and proven work ethic and resume filled with skills, knowledge, abilities and accomplishments. However, I struggled to find my place in a new professional world, despite being armed with my newly acquired skills. I redefined who I am and where I wanted to be, what I wanted to see and do, and how I wanted to look and act. But I still seemed to consistently miss the mark.

It is now that I would like to say to those 400+ companies, corporations, organizations and institutions that rejected me, "Thank you!" "Thank you for making me even more hungry and tenacious and to make me seek and follow my inner *Spirit* and *core genius*." Without your denials, I may be losing myself again in life's busy work and not my life's work.

By reading this book, you are a "person of possibilities", pushing for challenge, novelty, acceptance, connection and creative expression.

Challenge #1: If you are, were or will be in a position of screening prospects and you need to inform them that they did not make the cut, please do the next right thing. Pick up the telephone and call the prospect to "coach" them, no matter how insignificant you may think it may seem. Provide honest, genuine, constructive feedback. Take what you have learned here and from your life thus far, and decide and identify their core competencies, skills, abilities and qualifications. Pay it forward. Encourage them to follow their heart, no matter their current decision, circumstances or competencies. I know we live in a litigious world. You must join the movement to bring common sense into common practice, to help others always. Do the next right thing, as if it were your own kin. Please. You will feel so much more fulfilled and less stressed about denying them on the current vacancy or position.

Stop placing disempowering, limiting beliefs in the minds of your family, friends, fellows, constituents, customers, or colleagues. You have heard of the sayings, "Be careful of the ass you kick today, as you might have to kiss it tomorrow." "Don't burn any bridges." Stand tall. Take the high road. "It really isn't personal, unless you let it become so." "God (or universe) does have a plan." I say, "Find your spirit, core genius, and/or giving purpose the soonest you can and chase it with all of your heart." If so, there is no failure, but rather character building flashes.

I am proud to say that I served, for an abridged time, in the US Navy with my only regret not being able to fulfill my initial obligation of 6 years. My US Navy career plan was abruptly shattered when I sustained significant injuries in a 15-car pileup on Freeway 5, in San Diego, CA. I faced my mortality, 4 times within 120 seconds. You can read about that experience that helped transform me in my free book, _120 seconds_. You can download it for free from my website, mcginnisconsultinggroup.com. _120 Seconds_, will provide insights as to my passion to write on the topics that I research and pursue answers. While your life begins at birth, my life was transformed within 120 seconds. God does work in unique ways.

Very little is more disheartening and maddening than witnessing others' enthusiasm being bridled or halted by their disempowering or limitied thinking or beliefs. When you complete the series, you will be able to recognize, even during a simple conversation, at a minimum, one limiting belief. For me to sit back and to do nothing about it, is wrong. I was made for greatness, not comfort. My "why" is in helping others find their truest, highest self, and to live a fulfilling and empowering life. This book series is meant to be much bigger than me, my ego or my pride. It is meant to start a movement through transforming you to decide, identify and eliminate limiting or disempowering beliefs in your life and circles of influence. A world without limiting beliefs coupled with my drive and passion to rid the world of mediocrity, one person at a time, manifests or equals a world filled with happier, more productive and loving people. A happier planet. Not asking too much, is it? No. Don't worry about the how, just envision with me, a world as such. A world with minimal stress and conflict, with a laser like focus on worldly issues that are real life fears.

A world without limits **+** worldwide movement for positive change **=** a happier, healthier planet.

Your part in this incredible journey and movement must be built on trust, courage and passion. You nor I, do not know where it will end, or if it will ever end, but rather to start this transcendence like tidal wave to encompass the globe. The second part is not having you live a mediocre life but rather have you embrace your talents and gifts that you too must share with the world, now.

You may have reached the same point in your life, where you too realized that you have lived in fear and not fully, not lovingly and not near enough. This book series will empower you to remove and overcome **any** obstacles or challenges that you possess or may encounter. We all have limiting beliefs. We all experience cognitive dissonance. We all practice cognitive distortions. (We all will learn more in Chapter 4.)

When you are ready to change your life, read on...

By undertaking the challenge to read this book series, you are now a "student of excellence". You are committing to constant and never ending improvement, learning, accepting of coaching and advising, 100% of the time, in pursuit of excellence, not comfort. You were made for this -so let's begin your Journey of Self-awareness and positively transform and impact your entire world.

If not now, when?

Chapter 1

Limiting Beliefs

"When it gets darkest, the stars come out." Unknown.

Limiting: Serving to restrict or restrain. Restrain: To hold back from action, under control. Beliefs: Something believed; an opinion or conviction. Confidence in the truth or existence of something not immediately susceptible to rigorous proof. A thought that is repeated so frequently and with sufficient emotion attached to it; that you accept it as reality.

Limiting Beliefs: Limiting beliefs are the mental restrains holding you back from taking action due to a belief that you either learned, inherited, adopted and led to accept as fact.

You have a spirit or core genius within you. At first, it may be a challenging or difficult process: Defining and untwisting cognitive distortions; defining, identifying accepted or perceived rooted disempowering and limiting beliefs (that you may hold or have held for many years). Emotionally and mentally, you may likely feel exhausted having to go through the process. You may generate and experience feelings of regret, remorse, embarrassment and/or fear. You may generate and experience feelings of elation, relief, "aha" moments and laughter within the confusion.

Decide. Identify. Generate. Summon. D.I.G.S. The last two are to generate action and summon an affirmation that will keep you inspired and to make a concerted effort to advance internal healing. Before, during and even after you "D.I.G.S.", you must keep an open and growing mind and heart and to incessantly peel back the layers of clutter until the exact issue (belief/distortion) appears. You will forever more be continually growing, adapting and accepting clarity through action, by retraining your subconscious' habits and behaviors.

At times, it could be as easy as reading the different types of distortions or beliefs and making a conscious decision to stop it. At other times, it may seem like there are insurmountable odds at finding the root issue(s). It is the practice to be evaluating your situation and response levels daily.

I use a statement daily to assess a response:

"Upon objective review, is my emotional response and subsequent behavior congruent to the situation?"

This statement is an example of **E + R = O**. **E**vents + **R**esponses = **O**utcome. (Chapter 5)

The next time something negatively perceived happens, please recite this statement, and then slowly respond accordingly. You don't always have to have the last word or be *flip-off* the other person. In reading this book, you will learn about experiences and tools to relieve some of life's perceived stresses or experiences.

To many, this is simple common sense. However, it is not common practice. You too, need little "reminders" to keep you on track, to keep your goals and dreams in focus, to keep mental clarity and emotional positivity. There are far too many "wolves" looking to steal away your moments of joyfulness. Smile big. Sing-on. Grab life by the horns. You cannot sing if you are preoccupied, angry, upset or delirious. And, you cannot shake another's hand with a clenched fist.

"Knuckle-bumps" are not handshakes. Be the example. Choose the next right response and behavior. "Be the difference that makes the difference."

Emotions, memories and conscious thinking can be trained to stay positive. By reading this book, you are searching for answers and tools to help you stay positive, to learn, grow and conquer limiting and disempowering beliefs, cognitive distortions and to clear your mind of any limitations. By implementing what you learn plays a critical role in outcomes and happiness.

Limiting beliefs can be as simple as "I'm not good with money" to the more complex "Every time I make a change (in my life or career) something *bad* happens." There are an infinite number of limiting beliefs and I would guess that you could name at least 35 easily identifiable limiting beliefs in your life.

Exercise #1: List 5 limiting beliefs under each life area. I do not want to "limit" you, but to help you get started, here are some of the most common.

Financial: "The rich get richer while the poor get poorer."

Education: "I cannot afford to go to college." Or "I do not have the time for a Master's Degree."

Recreation: "I have a bad hip, I can't ski anymore."

Health/Body/Fitness: "I don't have time to eat right, work out regularly and maintain a FT job."

Relationships: "Let's just get the kids out of High School, then we will focus on "us"."

Personal/Spiritual: "If you believe, you will achieve." (Only if it is God's or the Universe's Plan!)

Contributions: "What do I have to offer, I am nobody special?"

The first 2-3 will be quick, but please sit back, close your eyes and generate 5 in each life area. Once you begin to understand what is limiting you in each life area, you will be able to spit out at least 5 more. Take the time NOW, to find a quiet place and D.I.G.S. There are no right or wrong answers.

What may appear real, is usually not the case. When a sage Monk was asked how he lives such a happy life, free of stress, he replied, "Real stress is when a rhinoceros is chasing you." You have experienced what perceived to be real stress, anxiety or fear. You generated these feelings. Was there a rhinoceros chasing you?

You may think it to be career suicide or even out of your circle of influence to approach your organization's CEO with an idea to improve a process. Subconsciously, you are generating this anxiety, stress and fear. But remember, they are a person just like you. Having the managerial courage and fortitude to approach the CEO to share your idea could be the missing puzzle piece their management team was seeking, but have not yet uncovered. You are important, your insights, answer or opinion counts, no matter your current circumstances or competencies.

You can list another dozen examples of cognitive delusions or wrongly formed paradigms. Have you ever just taken that leap of faith and reached out to someone with your idea? Have you ever just asked this person for a minute of their time, to save the organization money? Why not? Who said you cannot speak to them? This is a real example of a disempowering paradigm. Stop. Share. Signify your existence.

And don't let limiting beliefs take control of you. The time is now to choose the person you want to be from this point forward and how you will look, act, be and do in the following days, weeks, months, and years. Decide and define who you are and want to be. Don't allow others to define, box or paint you into a corner. Rid yourself of the proverbial paint brush. Rid yourself of doubts and fears.

Brendon Burchard often states, "The power plant does not have energy, it generates it." We all have our own internal power plant that produces 100% of our thoughts, feelings, behaviors, beliefs and values. 100%. You can choose to be sad, mad, angry and depressed or you can choose to be happy, vibrant, resilient, grateful and joyous.

When was the last time that you lived freely, with no worries? When was the last time you felt that moment of untarnished joy? You can now decide and identify disempowering or limiting beliefs, now is the time to generate massive action to remove all barriers to this peacefulness.

Nothing can be more disconcerting, than witnessing anyone, especially loved ones, placing themselves into a disempowering state of mind and being. These self-sabotaging people not only inflict suffering upon themselves but onto and into others.

This leads you to grasp why we have become a collection of adults where everything is wrong. Deny the mediocrity of the 93%. Commit to live like the 7%. Generate a life filled with joy, love, health and abundance. Rise and join in this movement to turn the irrational cognitive tide. It takes a village to raise a child. It takes one person to start a movement. It takes a vision, dream and passion to live life to your highest potential. Never give up. Never quit trying.

You may know of several other people that have faced certain death, and against all odds, survived. They survived this initial challenge. The most difficult battle is in how they will process, recover and grow from the challenge. Most will generate a strong association and overgeneralize any negative event in their life and link it to their experiences. They created an emotionally rooted, disempowering and syllogistic belief. A true cognitive distortion.

"Distortion-ists" generate, at the slightest sign of challenge, assumptive and maladaptive behaviors. It doesn't matter the circumstance, words or phrases, actions or people or attitudes combined with your lack of self-discipline to generate self-defeating behaviors that allow this distortion to continue, fester and grow. You are not living fully, you are living in fear. You accept and continue to generate fears on top of fears, deep inside of your subconscious mind, poised to spring to assumptions without facts. Stop. Quit. Don't do it. By dealing with these generated fears, courage will emerge. For without fear, courage cannot exist.

You have become a dream-killer, despite all that you have experienced and preached….

Survivors and victims of wars, conflicts, incidents, accidents, arguments or anxieties suffer from symptoms similar to Post Traumatic Stress Disorder (PTSD). The symptoms that generate or create limiting beliefs can be caught and eradicated, in 4 easy to remember steps.

D.I.G.S.

1. **D**ecide on making a change on a limiting belief, Thought or Action.

2. **I**dentify your Limiting Beliefs, Thoughts and Actions.

3. **G**enerate bold action by re-programming or re-training.

4. **S**ummon unrelenting positivity through affirmations of your new identity.

D.I.G.S. can be most fruitful in that it will spawn a healthy mind, body and soul. It is a simple and easy to remember acronym that you can apply to any thought, feeling, fear or unsettling behavior or experience. Feel free to use this as a tool in your arsenal of living your highest self.

I want to inspire you to take courageous action and commit to being extraordinaire or in the top 2% of your field or career. When this movement takes hold, we will quickly create the top 5%, then 10% and eventually, the top 25%. Imagine a world where there are 18% more extraordinaire people. In life, there are no ceilings. Potential is endless.

I am trusting that you are genuinely interested in gaining helpful insights into the secrets of mastering limiting beliefs and maximizing life's pleasures. To get the most out of this book is to have the *self-discipline* to complete the exercises to the best of your abilities. You cannot lose weight without exercise. You cannot grow properly if you don't exercise proper eating and sleeping habits. You cannot run a marathon if you don't practice. This holds true in personal and professional growth. You must complete the exercises to continue to learn and grow.

Daily Exercise: Using a scale of 1 to 10, rate yourself daily in all 7 life-areas. 1 being dismal or nonexistent and 10 being alive and vibrant. Start a journal. Each evening, just prior to retiring for the day/night, write down the following 7 life areas and rate yourself. Finances/Professional, Education/Self Improvement, Recreation/Hobbies, Health/Body/Fitness, Relationships/Family, Personal/Spiritual and Contributions/Legacy. In order to grow, you must be honest in all of your answers, 100% of the time. It is up to you if you chose to share these results with anyone else, but I would encourage you to set checkpoints, benchmarks and milestones with your loved ones. Positivity feeds on positivity. Each day the numbers will change in any area. It is about improving, working on balance and shooting for extraordinaire, not perfection. If you are all 1's, you are discrediting yourself. If you are all 10's, you are being egotistical. How do you rate? You are creating the new you. Behaving, doing and being your highest self.

Always do the next right thing, no matter the consequence or what people may think or do. Be honest and explicit with one another, not rude, but genuine, and watch how much more vibrant your life-areas will flourish and generate.

There are beliefs that are generated or are placed by either you or those around you. I am not implying that you or the company you keep are inadequate, unprofessional or incompetent. What I am implying is that it's become second nature to take the easiest or fastest route, to play the blame game or rush through your hectic, full schedule of patients, clients, friends and family. I have always shared with all of my team members the following quote, 'If the path you are taking is easy, maybe you are on the wrong path." Never settle for less than what you dream. I believe in having everyone, "Try harder." Start by being brutally honest with yourself. Competence = Confidence. Faith = Trust. Encourage = Growth.

Chapter 2

Authenticity and Self-Discovery

"To know oneself is to love oneself." unknown

Authenticity: Possessing the claimed or attributed character, quality, or origin, not counterfeit.

Self: A person or thing referred to with respect to complete individuality: one's own self.

The emphases in this book series is to be brutally honest with yourself always, no more excuses. "At the end of the day, let there be no excuses, no explanations, no regrets." Steve Maraboli

Discover and identify who you were, are and will be in __
years. Choose to start living freely, loving openly and
consciously generating new auto-responses, with your
highest self and giving purpose in mind.

This is all possible through free will and choice. You may not
know it, but you are in control of your thoughts, feelings,
emotions and behaviors. What you don't know is that your
body generates these. These are generated by your
subconscious and conscious minds. Your auto responses
are subconsciously driven where as your new responses will
be consciously driven or generated. It comes down to your
willingness to be your highest self always.

To practice and master self-discipline, when deciding how
you receive, interpret, and identify with your responses,
thoughts and processes. Consciously "checking-out" of a
situation, by asking yourself to rate how you are receiving
and reading the situation or event. Is this tiring? Yes. Is this
easy? No. By keeping a **healthy mind, energized body and
purpose driven soul**, your body will compensate, balance
and bring your body to expect this higher level of mental
engagement.

How do you really know who you are? When will you know,
you have found yourself? How? It is when you immerse into
the deepest part of *you*, most often, you will find and emerge
knowing the authentic you and what leaves you feeling
fulfilled. When you emerge from this deep contemplation and
learning, you will clearly see who you want to be, do, act and
play. With self- discipline comes clarity. With clarity comes
self-confidence. With self-confidence comes competence
and courage.

How do you go about immersing? There are many ways to
go into a deep sense of contemplation or immersion. You
can use the internet or ask people of possibility or your
influencers how or what they do to reach this inner balance
or centeredness. Not everybody will have a comfort level in

asking an influencer or person of possibility in fear of embarrassment. They are human, they will understand and if they don't, they will look to you as their influencer or person of possibility. You can also use a priest or religious leader, reputable therapist, psychologist, cognitive behavior therapist, or psychiatrist. Another way is by practicing disciplined, consistent prayer, meditation, listening, yoga, or a similar mental exercise. Most of today's leaders practice some sort of meditation. Some of the most level headed thinkers either pray or meditate, devotedly and consistently. They listen to their inner guidance system, aka voice of reason.

Will you always get it, right? Will you *always* know what to do about every social situation? Will you respond differently each time? Do you *always* become stronger when you are challenged? Have you come out of a challenge having not learned anything? Have you ever been so confused after a significant event in your life, you just don't know who you really are or were or where in the hell your response(s) came from?
The answers all lie within you. They can and will vary dependent upon these 4 main factors.

1. Physical presence.
2. Emotional presence.
3. Spiritual presence.
4. Mental presence.
5.

Presence: the ability to project a sense of ease, poise, or self - assurance, especially the quality or manner of a person's bearing before an audience. It means to be consciously and enthusiastically present with all senses with zero distractions.

You need to have a quiet mind, where nothing else in the world matters more than where you are now, physically, emotionally, spiritually and mentally (mindfulness). If you are not fully present, you are missing out on that moment and as mentioned before, you cannot get more time. Parents and Grandparents will often offer advice on how fast kids grow. With society as it is, "kids" are expected to grow up even faster, as society rushes everyone. Take back control and slow time. These kids have an infinite amount of the world's knowledge at their fingertips. Literally. However, they need to practice good physical, emotional, spiritual and mental presence and find a mentor, influencer or person of possibilities to provide wisdom and advice.

So much falls into being comfortable, confident and loving of yourself. The sooner you "D.I.G.S." the sooner you will become your highest performing self. Are you living to become the person *you want to become? Or* have you been living up to somebody else's expectations? Perhaps a parent, grandparent, leader, coach, teacher, sibling or an idol that has a stranglehold onto who you were or how they imagined. Maybe you have been driven (guided) by other's expectations and have not yet developed your own inner self. "Live your purposeful life, not a busy or undefined life."

In societies, all around the globe, pressures are extremely high as soon as you graduate to get out into the "real world", diving right in and start working. That is, until 20 years have passed and you waken and do not realize who you are or why you are working where you are. This is a somber reality for many. Please push for extraordinaire in everything that you do. Be the absolute best parent, grand parent, aunt, uncle, cousin, sibling, teacher, coach, trainer or religious leader.

When mentoring, or rearing anyone, be very conscious in what you say, do, act and teach. Maintain a list of absolutes or commandments that might include values, morals, religious beliefs, and the golden rules. Push for excellence in education. Defy the fact that teaching is one of the lowest paying jobs with the second most amount of influence. What should they be paid, or what is it worth to your child's future?

Words are so incredibly powerful. It is not easy being either a parent or a teacher. Teach those who you mentor to pay it forward, read a great book each week. Readers are leaders. Leaders have written goals. The rest work for those with written goals. No goal is too lofty. No dream is too outrageous. No passion is too much.

To know oneself is to truly and unconditionally love oneself. Have you ever allowed self-talk, you know, your "inner voice," to say nothing but positive comments? Or does your inner voice only criticize (you are your biggest and harshest critic, IF you allow it to be so)? "I am not smart enough." "I weigh too much" or as my friend Gred would say, "I am too short for my weight" I don't have the energy. I am not pretty. I cannot do that. I was born poor. I am too young. I am too old. I am too _____. Have you ever heard this voice inside of you? Stop it.

Stop it by replacing your negative self-talk with positive affirmations, dreams, passions, and goals along with checkpoints, benchmarks and milestones. If you have access to a computer, search for positive affirmations. Search the web for free guided meditation, search the web for limiting beliefs, cognitive distortions, cognitive dissonance and congruency. You will be amazed at the sheer amount of time, energy and research that has been achieved thus far in these areas.

Challenge yourself to push even these beliefs that you read to add even more. And, you quickly realize that you are not alone. Starting now, recognize this inner voice. Find, construct or generate positive affirmations, wake 15 minutes earlier, get ready, sit down with some headphones, listen and recite these positive affirmations, religiously and daily. To the point that if you do not do it, you feel "off" or "awkward" as you stumble into your day, week, month, or year.

Jack Canfield has his audiences recite a lot of positive affirmations. One of my most favorite, widely used and recommended: "No matter what you say or do to me, I am still a worthwhile person." And Les Brown's, "No matter how bad it is or how bad it gets, I am going to make it." And another, "Try Harder" by John Paul Getty. There are literally millions. Choose your top 3-5 and affirm your self-esteem, confidence and watch your life grow. Focus on the positive, find the silver lining in everything – no matter how dark or unknowingly it might seem.

"There will always be laughter after pain. There will always be sunshine after rain." Matthew Kelly.

Try quoting your mentor, Canfield, Brown, Getty or Kelly the next time someone calls you a name, throws you the middle finger, attempts to put you down, cuts you off mid-sentence, or embarrasses you. Just recite this over and over either aloud (if alone) or in your head. It works either way, but, has so much more impact when you recite it to yourself in the mirror each morning and night. Try this for the next 30 days. Write down your favorite quote or what I have shared here, on a notecard. Let me know how that works for you. Remember, you can neither wish nor think yourself into something you are not, without bold and massive action.

If only more people would use this, I know it would cut down on road rage, outbursts at home, work or play. It is scientifically proven that you cannot hold two opposing moods at the same time. It does take more muscles in the face to frown than to smile, this will help with your newly found fatigue. Be Brave. Be Bold. Be You.

Have you ever tried to do something and you hear a voice in your head advising otherwise?
If not, you need to listen, as it is your voice of reason or as I mentioned before in this book, we are all born with an inner spirit or core genius. This can also be called your internal GPS (Global Positioning System). It does not matter who

you claim as your creator, we all have an inner voice. When you love yourself, absolutely and unconditionally, it is truly amazing the weight that is lifted off of your shoulders. "I am the one who had the yoke on my shoulders and yet did not know it, I was blind." Magnificent Year of Mercy Companion

In a survey of 600 university students, they were asked to name their biggest problem. 450 of the students replied, "Lack of self-confidence." I wonder where the remaining 150rated their lack of self-confidence. Second? Third? Wherever it was rated, if they lacked self-confidence at all, their education would do them little good. Why? Dr. Walter Scott, President of Northwestern University said, "Success or failure is caused more by mental attitudes than by mental capacities." What kind of "attitude" do you have? No amount of education will help unless you truly practice "(intense) believing" then you will justly succeed. If you have positively focused beliefs and self-discipline, no matter your current circumstances or competencies, you will achieve whatever you clearly define as a goal. Visualize with such intensity, that you know how it looks, tastes, smells, feels and sounds.

"As a man thinketh, so is he." Proverbs 23:7 "Without a vision, you will perish." Anonymous.

Many others have gone on to say, in so many terms, "You become what you think about most of the time." If you are constantly worrying about money, you will get more of what you are thinking. If you are constantly living in fear, you will live life in a cage or shell. What are your thoughts? Positive and uplifting, intently and unwaveringly? Many have gone on to say, that the "Law of Life" (Law of Attraction) is that (intense and clear) **belief** attracts to it all the elements which make its realization possible.

Yet, so many of us continue to carry on through our life, failing to decide, define and pursue your goals with clarity and belief in even yourself. There was another survey taken where almost nine out of ten people confessed that they suffered from feelings of inferiority and inadequacy.

Mathematically, this figures congruently, as 93% of society is not "happy" with their life. This is reasonably disheartening and quite scary. It is no wonder you have so many people sitting around passing gossip, rumors, pleading for more. Folks, the welfare train is on course to wreck in the USA. It is time to wake up, take focus and set sail to pursue a life filled with purpose, love, health and abundance. Will it be easy? Hell no. Will it take time? Yes. So get started immediately. What is your New Year's Resolution? What did you give up for Lent? What are your 7 life-area goals for this day, week, month, year, decade or life? How are you doing?

First thing you must **D**ecide, **I**dentify and **G**enerate the ability to sell <u>you</u> to <u>yourself</u>! If you cannot do this, you will never sell others on you or your ideas to anyone else, ever. Look, talk, act and **S**ummon your highest self, coupled with an intense belief that **you** are a success and **you** will be a success. "Act as if…"

I have 6 brothers and in the Summer of 2015, our brother Kevin spent 10 days canoeing in the Boundary Waters between Canada and the United States with a group of friends. He left his smartphone and as he said it, "…unplugged for the entire 10-day trip." He was astonished at how much more refreshed and focused he was upon his safe return. Be like my brother and unplug for 10 consecutive days. I will guarantee that if there is something so important that you had to be contacted, the other party will find a way.

There are real life and death emergencies, so I understand if you want to leave a contact number or share your itinerary with family and friends, so long as there is no communication unless absolutely warranted. In my brother's case, there were no electronic media or communications and had something happened to our Mom or anyone, he would have found out after he returned. Thank God nothing happened, so we didn't have to put good 'ole Mom on ice for a week. Just kidding Mom, love you.

There is so much more to life than watching cats do, well, whatever it is cats do on YouTube or compulsively attached to social media or having the overwhelming feeling or self-obliging feeling of never being able to miss out on anything. This constant sense of obligation and state of mind will burn you out, and quickly. You were not made to be chained to technology. Technology within communications is to be used as a tool, not the means to the end. However common and widely used, the overuse and even replacement of traditional technology is becoming commonplace and faceless in true, authentic human interpersonal communications. As mentioned earlier, you don't have to have the last word or wave, likewise, you don't have to be the first to hear, see, do, or be everything and everywhere.

When you have self-confidence, self-control and the self-discipline to say, "No" to those things that are not getting you closer to being the "perfect you", you will experience a state of unbridled freedom. If it is so important and it affects you, you will hear about it. Too many lack the self-control to not be the first to know about everything. Chances are high that life will continue without you being online or available 24/7. Take time to find, practice, hone and re-brand who you are and want to be. No more mind control games or technological leashes. Cut the cord, like the doctor did when you were born. Be free. Be bold. Be who you want to be.

Exercise #2: Take (at least) one day each month, from midnight to midnight, where you are free from any electronic-tethers, spouses, partners, family, and friends and do something for just yourself. Go on a nature hike, walk, ride or a stay-cation where you don't leave town but are still alone. Take time(s) throughout the 24 hours to rate, on a scale of 1 – 10. how you are doing in all areas of your life: Finances/Professional, Education/Self Improvement, Recreation/Hobbies, Health/Body/Fitness, Relationships/Family, Personal/Spiritual and Contributions/Legacy. On a scale of 1 – 10. Do it now. Practice mindfulness. (Chapter 8)

Technology is an amazing and evolving race. It is technology within social mediums, if not used in moderation, which is assassinating human communications as it was created and known. Acronyms, abbreviations, texting, snap chatting, tweeting, chirping, whatever, all removes us from our physical being and "self". Disagree? Then why is it so easy to text, tweet, snap chat or email someone a note "discussing" a difficult topic, that really needs to be done during a face to face conversation?

Because we allow fears to get in our way. Fear of how the person will feel, react, look or do, or the fear of how we will feel or react to them when they may resist. Stop.

Communications is at least two way, especially face to face. We feel it is easiest to send a difficult topic note as opposed to a face to face visit, because it is "convenient" "easy" but it is faceless and cowardly. Wake up. Do you not see human communications being assaulted and killed? As of 2023, technology still cannot feel or replace the genuine feelings of human connection and belonging.

Experts have found that in communications, 7% is done with words, 38% with tonality (voice inflections), and a staggering 55% with body language (body positioning, eyes, arms and stance). Are you afraid of communications, rejection or embarrassment? If not, then do the next right thing, talk to people face to face. Save frustrations. Save communications. Save humanity.

While the internet is going to stick around, it is more important to learn, experience and share human interaction, connection and communications even more so today. You still get hired by a face to face interview, you still go on dates in person, and you still show affection to another person, with a gentle touch, an assuring hug or a soft kiss. Technology lacks presence. Technology lacks emotion (not emoji-cons). Technology lacks spirituality. Technology lacks sense of appreciation. Technology lacks sense of belonging. Technology lacks in human connection. Technology is faceless and removes authentic emotions and feelings, Technology is being used for the worst: killing, bombing, spying, stealing identities and pornography. In real life, You Only Die Once. YODO. And it is final. Period. You cannot "re-generate" or start over with a click of a button.

Technology is destroying the sanctity of marriage, trust, relationships and love. Please take a moment and think about how you may be using "technology". Now, would you do the exact same thing if your mother or father were in the same room observing you? If you are not ashamed would you download in front of your spouse, family or friends, would you be using technology the same way? Technology will forever evolve and with it will pose more and more threats to authentic human communications, feelings and behaviors.
Don't lose yourself in technology. Lose yourself in your life's work.

Speaking of loss, did you know that the average American watches 4 hours of television a day? That's over **60 days** per year. How many books could you read in 60 days? How many more memories could you be creating and enjoying with family and friends in 60 days? How much more could you be generating and contributing to the world in these 60 days?

Challenge #2: How many books can you read in the next 60 days, 4-6-8-10? Set a goal and please let me know. How much better do you feel after reading a book versus watching a movie? Which provides you with more pleasure or knowledge, and less commercials? I know that you will notice an immediate difference in communications and very quickly. You will also live more freely and with much less self-inflicted or generated stresses.

We need to SLOW DOWN time. It "happens" all the time during times of crisis or a life and death situation. It happened to me during my car accident. Everything seems to happen in slow motion. What would it feel, look, taste, sound or smell like if time moved this slowly permanently? We didn't know any differently, but were much more mindful of not only ourselves, but others as well. Take the time to absorb the beauty, listen to nature's wondrous concert of different "instruments" (animals and wind).

We all have become too lax in taking self out of control, discipline, confidence and competence.
By dropping "self" before so many powerful words, not only removes responsibility, but more importantly, it robs us of many opportunities for growth and contribution.

We drop "self" and imply that it's society's worry to make it right, fair or equal. Entitlements, handouts and expectations have become commonplace. Worse yet, relativism is trying to become the norm. The time is _now_, to put your**self** back into these roles. Take absolute and full responsibility for everything in your life. I take it to the extreme at times, for example, on the days that I fail to hit my daily, biking, miles per hour goal, I will say, "I just lack the self-discipline to maintain my rotations per minute. I need to push myself harder, 100% of the ride." If we are being completely honest, the removing self theory is true, right?

In life, you take away things you cannot experience through technology. I am not sure if it is due to just technology or if it is in the use of acronyms, abbreviations, shortcuts, feelings of having a lack of time or is it laziness and our inability to accept one**self.** Is it in having a lack of discipline, denying ownership or responsibility? How many other "self" words are there that we make faceless and remove ownership? Self-esteem. Self-confidence. Self-existent. Self-reliance, Self-help. Self-initiated. Self-less. Self-made. Self-restraint. Self-satisfied. Self-starter. Self-sufficient. Self-taught and self-validation. I think you get the point. Take ownership see how it improves your life, relationships and contributions to the world.

Chapter 3
Fears
"Fears and the Inner Voice"

<u>Fear</u>: A distressing emotion aroused by impending danger, evil, pain, whether the threat is real or imagined; the feeling or condition of being afraid.

As a child, I remember learning how to swim and advancing through the different levels each summer. I vividly remember taking one level that required jumping off the 12' high-dive board. At the time, my fear absolutely felt real, inherited or learned, I was scared. Why? I had never fallen from 4 feet let alone volunteering to leap from 12 feet. Regardless, there was a fear growing and about to erupt via my esophagus, with each step up the ladder leading to the infamous 12' high-diving board. Limiting belief? Yes. Inherited? No. Learned? Yes. Thank you, Mom.

The limiting belief or fear, was more than the leap of faith or the fall itself. Looking back and squeezing myself into those same swimming trunks, I can remember thinking, "I just cannot do this, I am afraid of heights. I will get knocked out when I hit the side of the pool, or worse yet, the concrete under the diving board. Then I will have the embarrassment of the lifeguard diving in to save me. Or having to call the ambulance, and I know that my brothers are watching and laughing. Hell, my mom is down there watching, and she has never done this!"

Was the fear real or imagined? Imagined. It was taking all the information that I received from my family and peers growing up, interpreting it as a real fear reinforced by my mom that it is scary.

I remember beating myself up with negative self-talk and then taking the courageous initiative of facing my peers and worse yet, younger kids, as I did the walk of shame back to the ladder and climb down to safety. After a lot of cajoling and laughter from everyone, I found myself standing at the end of the diving board again. The act of standing so far above the water wasn't scaring me, it was the insecurity felt during the fall, having my stomach contents in my throat, the feeling of embarrassment, and all of this was imagined.

This same fear stops so many of us from taking the proverbial leap of faith in our personal and professional lives. The knot in our stomach induces fear – fear of losing that sense of security, financially, emotionally and physically – creating doubt and limiting beliefs that you could lose everything if you leave your job.

I wish I could report that my fears of heights and deep water were over, but they were not, not quite yet. I know now, that fears are learned, they are not biologically passed onto or transmitted via the umbilical cord into you. However, my fears were once again rearing its ugly head nearly 10 years later, after having passed all of the swimming lessons and 12' high dives.

When I was around 15 years old, on one of two canoe trips made to the Boundary Waters (Minnesota, USA and Canada) we would stop each night, always picking the "perfect campsite." Perfect meaning that it had *perfect* cliffs for jumping into the water to wash off the day's sweat and toil. Despite my prior successes, my inner voice was once again saying, "I cannot do this, I am afraid of heights." Well, after much coaxing and mocking from my so-called friends, I made the hike up the hill, as my heart started pounding like a drum, gasping to catch my breath, knees getting weaker by the step, almost like I was climbing Mount Everest or someplace similar.

I knew this was surely the prelude to my most certain death. 45 minutes later, and it wasn't so much the 2-minute walk to the top, but 43, agonizing and grueling minutes of knee-shaking, heart pumping, dry-heaving, sweating and frothing feeling in my mouth. I stood and watched the others jumping and screaming, laughing and surviving the jump. I didn't wait in line, but stood to the side, weighing my options and humiliations in not jumping, when all of sudden, and from deep inside my earlier sickened belly, came this eruption of courage as I heard myself yell out, "I love you Mom and Dad!" and I jumped as far out into the sky as I possibly could. At that very point, all I had, was faith and belief in the survival stories from the fools afore me. What lasted maybe10 seconds, felt like 2 minutes, as time once again slowed for me. One second I remember my feet on the rocks and thorns, the next second, I felt the sting of the water on the bottoms of my feet as cool, refreshing, crystal clear water swallowed me.

I survived the jump! Feelings of joy, courage and accomplishment were quickly overshadowed by yet another fear, "Now I was going to drown!" "I am 15 feet beneath the surface." "What the hell did I do? Will I be missed? Who gets to carry my body over the portages back to the main camp? Will they just feed me to the bears? Then as quickly as the impact, I crested the water's edge and was welcomed by laughter, cheers and jeers. I did it! I lived! I fought the law (of fear) and the law didn't win.

All the while, my subconscious had flashed stories from my upbringing that heights and deep waters were dangerous and will result in death, period. These long-standing limiting beliefs or fears that were deeply rooted inside of me, were washed away in a matter of a minute after taking bold action. I hold no fear of heights or deep waters. While fears may disappear for you as they did for me that day, life is full of challenges, opportunities and character building moments. They will last more than a minute or if you hold tight. Were my fears real or perceived?

"To have no fear, is to know fear." Dr. Michael H.

Wishing and thinking will not change or eliminate fears or limiting beliefs as much as acting or better yet, bold action, it is so incredibly powerful and gratifying. Action turns into momentum reinforcing new, positive beliefs and providing intensifying courage so that your dreams and goals are realized. Goal setting takes on a new meaning when there are no limiting beliefs or standards. Try it. Track it. Transcend yourself.

Exercise #3: Quickly write down 3-5 fears that you hold and may or may not have shared. How do you feel after writing down these truths? Now, rank these fears on a scale of 1 – 10. 1 holding little significance in your life and 10 strangling you from personal and professional growth. Do it now. Be honest. Be genuine. Be freed!

Feel the feelings associated. Feel the sense of release, gratification and accomplishment by just admittedly releasing these from your subconscious to your conscious mind. Begin now to be that new "you."

"People may think you have achieved a great deal but the truth is You know that you are still operating well below your potential.

Could it be because you have never really taken that leap of faith?" -Matthew Kelly

Take your leap of faith to follow that special person, dream job, your heart or to quench that burning desire or spirit deep within you. A sense of faith tied to your internal GPS-spirit, to guide you, along with your inner voice of reason. Chances are, that you have already taken a leap of faith, for example, when your state of mind was altered by excitement, love, novelty and challenge. Yet, as you gain more life experience, you take fewer and fewer leaps of faith. Why is this? Are you no longer seeking challenge, novelty or change? Are you living comfortably? Or are you living in fear? Are you settling for complacency? Some will realize, after several decades, life is too short to live other than abundantly and with genuine gratitude. No matter how old you get, gravity stays the same. Stand tall. There will always be laughter after pain and there will always be sunshine after the rain. There are only two certainties in life: death and taxes. Fear neither for they are inevitable and unpredictable. Dare. Dream. Develop new hobbies.

You have free will. You have the freedom of choice. You are your own generator. You generate all your own feelings. In every moment of every day, you subconsciously go on auto pilot in your own little world. When life is passing by without a second thought. Life goes as fast or as slow as you decide it to be so. The more presence you generate, the slower time will go. You have experienced the sense of time change at some point in your life. It is always during a highly motivated or emotional time. Life seems to go into slow motion during these heightened levels of emotion. Unfortunately, you have allowed time to pass and have played it "safe" your entire life, by trusting in cognitive delusions, disempowering, learned beliefs like fear, regret, and resentment.

You are playing it safe regarding living a confined or comfortable life, never truly pushing yourself for the betterment of contribution. How much more could you have given in the past? Really. Well, it doesn't matter now as you cannot change the past, no matter how hard you try. You can generate emotions and actions in the present by referring to lessons from your past and set goals and dreams for your future. Do not try to live in the past or in the future. You only get one chance in each moment, then it too passes, either consciously or subconsciously (auto-responses). Don't live an unexamined life. Take control. Take bold action. Summon your affirmations.

What matters now is how you choose to live life. May I suggest you identify several goals as well as one audacious (life changing) goal in all 7 life-areas. If you haven't yet, start a bucket list, with zero limiting beliefs or perceived fears. Do it now. Do it for your family. Do it for your generation. Do it for your legacy.

If you continually worry and fear about the lack of money, the Law of Attraction will listen and give you more fear, worry and lack of money. Push yourself. Dream big. It takes as much energy to dream big as it does to dream small. My mother always said, "Dream big, it's free!' Moms know best.

Everyone has 100 excuses and answers but no good reason. You choose to lack willpower or self-discipline to stick to your diet, budget, relationship, career advancement, hobby, faith and contribution. Commit, right now, to turning your negative self-talk to only positive self-talk. (Self-talk is the babble you have echoing in your head, all day, every day.)

You have or had aging parents, grandparents, relatives, friends, whomever. Did it not bother you too, that as soon as their life-calendar clock hit a certain age, they chose to change? Change in the case of stop doing the activities they loved to do or dreamt of doing. Don't allow the aging process, societal habits and fears change your course of action by accepting, endorsing and reinforcing these and other limiting beliefs. Don't become an armchair cowboy, critiquing and criticizing (excuses) in why you didn't do something. Admit that you too have fears, but are going to become an active participant, to share in life's great experiences. Begin now by taking 100% responsibility for your life. Be active. Be bold. Be courageous. Be not afraid.

Start a movement with your family, friends, colleagues and others on healthy living. Start practicing what you preach, and becoming who you want to be. Your body (brain or mind included) is the most important tool that you will ever own. There are no returns, just free will and choice. Your body is constantly rebuilding, repairing and reproducing new cells to the point that you have rebuilt yourself every 7 years. How old are you? Are you limiting your activity based on your calendar age? What's holding you back from reaching your highest ability and purpose? Excuses? Reasons? Answers? Surround yourself with positivity, gratitude and optimism. There are hundreds of stories about people that started living after 60 calendar years. Colonel Harland Sanders was 61 when he started the KFC Franchise. J.R.R. Tolkien was 62 when the Lord of the Rings books hit the shelves. Ronald Reagan was 69 when he became President of the United States. Jack Lalanne, on his 70th birthday, handcuffed and shackled, swam and towed 70 rowboats with an average person per rowboat, 70 total people. (The exercise called "Jumping Jack" was named after Jack Lalanne.) Nelson Mandela was 76 when he became President. You choose your limits, if any. Choose with free will and imagination. Choose now who you want to be in X years.

Fears and limiting beliefs are reinforced through subconscious responses. Mental conditioning and broadening at all ages is essential. No matter your choice, make a lifelong commitment to never quit learning. Challenge your fears. Challenge your mind. Challenge yourself to read one book each month, then each week. After 2 years of reading one book per week, it is comparable to a Bachelor's Degree. Some experts have claimed that you are considered an "authority" if you have read 12 books on a subject. Be creative. Be loved. Be smarter. Be a genius.

Fears, beliefs and the aging process are inevitable. When living a life of expectations of others and not for yourself, you will be short-tempered, impatient, caged, complacent and compliant. It is because you are not living for yourself, you are living for somebody else. Begin now to live the life God has envisioned for you.

You fear that if you live the life that you want or dream that you might upset or hurt feelings. If they love you, they will allow you to push yourself to follow your purpose, mission, passions and dreams. Up to this point, whatever the good excuses (lies) that you have told or tell yourself, you will never be truly free and feeling fulfilled. Soon you will have reunions and wonder what happened to you. You have accepted limiting beliefs, fears and doubts to maintain control of your subconscious. You have allowed yourself to be stripped of so many possible, positive memories and incredible times. Live without regrets, resentment or retirement. Become your best, beginning now. Conquer your negative thoughts and you will become who you desire.

You have nearly 60,000 thoughts a day. Of these, most feed the "negative wolves" with more than 50,000 of these thoughts. Which wolves are you feeding? Can you imagine your potential if you were to feed to the "good wolves" 50,000 thoughts a day? How would this change your outlook on life, friendships, intimacy, joy, productivity or gratitude? How would you live your life if you knew you were dying in 12 months? Live life now with that same passion and level of acceptance.

Go visit someone in a nursing home, hospice center, pediatric ward or someone you know who is terminally ill. Ask them what they would do differently? You will not find anyone that wishes they had one more day to work. There will always be the dream killers, but more so, there exists a sense of positivity in the room, and despite nearing the end, these people are positive, upbeat and laughing as much as possible. Laughter helps in acceptance. Laughter helps in healing. Laughter helps to keep you feeding the right wolves. Believe it. Try it. Don't wait.

Maybe you have a fear of speaking in front of groups or singing outside the safety of the shower or bedroom walls. Maybe you have a fear of the dark, confined spaces, spiders, bugs or whatever. You generate these fears. Conquer these fears and see how it improves your life. What doesn't kill you, makes you stronger, really. You can go on living in fear your entire life, or, you can self-educate, create your own beliefs, and produce many phenomenal memories along the way. Fear is a learned behavior. Defeat it. Defy it. Deny fear through bold and courageous action.

Chapter 4
Congruency, Cognitive Dissonance & Distortions

Congruency: is the quality of state of agreeing or corresponding.

Cognitive Dissonance: is the state of having inconsistent thoughts, beliefs, or attitudes, especially relating to behavioral decisions and attitude change.

Cognitive Distortions: are simply ways that our mind convinces us of something that isn't true. These inaccurate thoughts are usually used to reinforce negative thinking or emotions — telling ourselves things that sound rational and accurate, but only serve to keep us feeling bad about ourselves.

To be congruent in your actions and beliefs is not easy. Ever. The cognitive dissonance is the discomfort you feel when you are not acting or behaving in alignment with your morals, values and beliefs. This becomes very taxing and draining of our energy reserves and creates more stress. Cognitive Distortions are the negative thinking and emotions that one negative or doubting inner voice is telling us, to be real beyond rationale. It is the diagnosis or categorizing your life's perceptions of reality.

No matter your age, you have your own belief and values system that was "inherited" or invoked from your parents, grandparents, relatives and others as you progressed through and beyond your developmental years, to this point. After all, aren't you merely extensions of those who have taught or inspired you throughout your life? There are times often in your life when you must decide: Change or More of the same (Same Shit Different Day: "SSDD")? Perhaps, you are there now. What will you choose? You don't have to wait until a New Year, New month, New Week or the proverbial, Tomorrow I will start…. If not now, when?

For example, I was raised in a small town in South Dakota. There were (are) a lot of farming, manufacturing, blue and grey collared jobs and so the general rational, with so many of my classmates and friends, was to either go to work right out of High School or more schooling, pursuing your interests.

They say hindsight is 20/20 and many of us wish we knew then what we know now. For me, looking back over my lifetime by immersing myself in my daily exercises and meditations today, I realize the power and control of the mental tension that prevailed in anticipation of graduating high school. I was conflicted in either attending college, working or go see the world via the Military. With mounting angst in which to choose, I chose to join the US Navy at age 17, with my father's signature, in the delayed entry program.

This way, I released (ran from) the tension of choosing which way to go. I don't regret my volunteering. I could open my world much more quickly and see both coasts of the USA and could float the Pacific Ocean to witness some of the most incredible images the freedom and openness of the oceans provides. From sunrises and sunsets to the peacefulness and volatility the ocean can muster. How beautiful.

As you have read, God or the universe had a different plan for me. Unexpectedly and against my career plans, my time with the US Navy ended quickly and far too soon. All because two automobile drivers lacked self-control and self-discipline. This changed my course in life within 120 seconds. Please read my free story on my website, mcginnisconsultinggroup.com titled: "120 seconds." Please don't drive under the influence, ever. Stay in charge using self-control, self-discipline and human decency. Do not become a dream killer.

Today, I am doing my own physical therapy by exercising regularly, however, I still live in fear and pain. I practice forgiveness, prayer and meditation, but, up until recently, I have never admitted to living in fear since that accident. This was identified through deep contemplation, study and coaching from an influential people of possibility, like Dale Carnegie, Brendon Burchard, Jack Canfield, Stephen Covey, Jeffrey J Fox, Brene' Brown and many others. Thank you for all your secondary and worthy education through your books, videos and seminars.

However, I credit the US Navy, doctors, therapists and others for pushing me. I was pushed to accept beliefs beyond my control. I have used these "limiting beliefs" to become the person that I am today. Without experiencing all of the things that I did in the US Navy, I may not be writing about this topic today. Thank you to the US Navy and the Veterans Administration for providing me with the relentless challenges. I have lived, learned and leveraged so much over the past decade.

Lastly, come to think of it, I forgive all of you, who were not your best versions of yourself that day. I guess I never have "released" that thought, feeling or memory. I have carried this burden in my subconscious, and have never shared it with my immediate or extended family and friends. So much internal pressure, I finally burst into writing about it. I am grateful and appreciative for my time thus far and look forward to many more challenges that lie in wait for me and my family. Again, I forgive you. Do you see how easy it is to forgive?

I am just a guy, a human being that was muddling my way through life and made (make) plenty of errors by accepting and capitulating limiting beliefs and cognitive distortions. However, I am much more attuned to these powerful and truly limiting or disempowering beliefs.

You may by able to forgive people a bit easier now, but still have a difficult time forgetting. As I have shared, you are a student first and foremost. I am still identifying and consciously working to remove all the limiting beliefs tied to my accident and the nearly impassable challenges that I have faced thus far. Choices, both consciously and unconsciously are controlled by your fears turned into thoughts and actions.

Your choice to "hang out" with a certain type of people, either the positive and inspiring or the negative and resentful will also decide your actions, beliefs, and character. The mind is so incredibly complex and powerful. We still do not know the full potential of our brain. However, until you truly find your internal plumb line or center and find your inner peace, you will continually be replaying these damaging beliefs in your mind, over and over and over. You must act. You must do the next right thing. You must become vigilante.

You must also become extraordinaire in identifying, defining, uprooting limiting beliefs and have an inpentrable commitment to release any restraining beliefs, incongruences, cognitive dissonance and distortions to find your truest and highest self and living in genuine harmony and tranquility. You already have, once, when you were in those moments of pure and unaltered moments of joyfulness as a child. Find that version.
Live up to your highest self: Live. Love. Laugh.

And regarding Limiting Beliefs: Decide. Identify. Abolish.

When I was presented with the shear reality that I was not going to walk again, open a door without assistance, and having to be a burden on my already financially strapped parents of 7 children, I knew that I was created for much greater, healthier times. These limiters, in addition to new and disempowering limits and distortions were weighing me down in all 7 life areas. I tried to overcompensate by being somebody that I wasn't. I compartmentalized feelings and emotions. I was living not only in fear, but living my life safely by being meek, timid and tender.

Parents are always making sure that our children are hanging out with the right group of kids, so that they have another positive, reinforcing system in place. For the most part and depending upon your culture, you affect and have influence over your children the first 12-14 years. After this point, they start to look to peers for input, insights, behaviors, attitudes and dreams. They will come to you on a few things, however, the bulk of their informative opinions are brought out by the company they keep. Find the influencers and people of possibility in your school, work, career or religious institution. Be like them. Be who you want. Be who you want to become. Soon.

Against medical diagnosis, I chose to walk again. How? By using my own system: D.I.G.S. Decided not to accept a label/ limiting belief. Identified the MD's diagnosis as a limiting belief. Generated bold action, despite "the odds" and real pains. Summoned a positive outcome of me walking again by generating visualizations and reinforcing them through consistent practice, until I achieved success. I visualized mountain biking, riding horses, playing sports and even officiating my favorites.

They say if you don't like what you see, step right up and do it yourself. Having no regrets or limited beliefs, I found myself umpiring baseball, from little league to amateur baseball. I hurt by the end of the first few innings, but, I tried harder, focused on the game and not myself. I had overcome a lot to get to this point. The reward of action far outweighed the pain that ensued. I have truly lived a "secretive" life by not sharing my story, my passions. That is, until now, when I have taken bold, massive action to share not only my story, passions and D.I.G.S. system, but to confess that despite all that I have overcome, I still live in fear.

At this point, I am strong in my faith, morals, beliefs and values. I am not saying that anyone who is a paralytic or worse, ought to be walking. However, I have met several people who are in wheelchairs, as they were told that they would end up in one "…sooner or later..." Now, these friends had crippling diseases and yes, the chances were strong that they would be in a wheelchair. Often people stop fighting and accept an idea, diagnosis and limiting belief without challenging or questioning it. Those feelings, fears or diagnosis carry a massive cloud of doubt and self-pity. This often leaves many to ask, "Why?" You may or may not ever find the answer to your question. You need to realize that it will not change things if you do find out the answers. Yes, it might make you a motivator and inspirer, but will it change the outcome? Stand tall. Fight hard. You choose when it is time to "roll."

When I visited with one person that was faced with a crippling disease and already, early in the diagnosis, choose to roll and not fight. This chafed my hide. I tried coaching him in how he still had time to do so much more beyond accepting the limiting distortion of "everybody will end up in a wheelchair." He just had to choose to live life more fully. He had to choose not to accept the limiting belief and distortions associated with the "norm". It was my "job" to coach him to learn from my story and experiences. While it did not change anything, he did continue driving his car, but not walking.

I did my best, with what I had in my arsenal of knowledge. It was at this defining moment that I realized my passion. To find, learn and coach. While it has taken me more than 8 years to read, research, practice and realize my gifts, I know that there isn't anyone that can tell you what you can or cannot do with your life's passions and Gifts inside of you. Follow your heart. Do what makes you happy. Find a way to make money while doing what you enjoy, are passionate about and what drives you to get out of bed each day. You can start by using the systematic "D.I.G.S." to find what you seek.

You can go ahead and try, but, after 40+ years of living life by other's expectations, I am giving you a head start. There are so many people, 93% of adults, who are not happy. Do you think they are all positive and supportive of your ideas and dreams? Hell no.

You have the power to imagine and visualize who you want to be, how you want to look, act, react and handle money. It is when you are not behaving, making opposing choices, whatever the case, this is when you get uncomfortable within yourself or as I call it, you are feeling incongruent. You have identified some limiting beliefs in your 7 life-areas. Now it is time to understand cognitive distortions.
There are generally the top 10-15 cognitive distortions. As identified and defined by Dr. David D. Burns, they are, in no order:
Personalization and Blame; All or nothing thinking; Jumping to conclusions, Overgeneralization, Emotional Reasoning, Labeling, Mental filtering, Should statements, Discounting the positives and Magnification or Minimization.

Let us take a closer look at these:
Personalization and Blame: You blame yourself for something you weren't entirely responsible for, or you blame other people and overlook ways that your own attitudes and behavior might contribute to a problem.

All or nothing thinking: You look at things in absolute, black and white categories.

Jumping to conclusions: (A) Mind reading – you assume that people are reacting negatively to you when there's no definite evidence for this; (B) Fortune Telling – you arbitrarily predict things will turn out badly.

Overgeneralization: You view a negative event as a never-ending pattern of defeat.

Emotional Reasoning: You reason from how you feel "I feel like an idiot, so I really must be one." Or "I don't feel like doing this, so I'll put it off."

Labeling: You identify with your shortcomings. Instead of saying, "I made a mistake," you tell yourself, "I'm a jerk," or "a fool," or "a loser."

Mental Filter: You dwell on the negatives and ignore the positives.

"Should Statements": You criticize yourself or other people with "Should" or "Shouldn'ts," "Musts," Oughts," "Have to-s" are similar offenses.

Discounting the positives: You insist that your accomplishments or positive qualities "don't count."

Magnification or Minimization: You blow things way out of proportion or you shrink their importance inappropriately.

Copyright 1980 by David D. Burns, M.D. Adapted from Feeling Good: The New Mood Therapy (New York: William Morrow & company, 1980; Signet, 1981)

Exercise #4: Re-read each of the cognitive distortions. Write down a time when you have experienced each distortion. Everyone has, frequently and too often experience cognitive distortions. If you come up with more than one, please write them down too. Write as many as you can think about, as this book is genuinely about helping you **D**ecide, **I**dentify, **G**enerating bold action and **S**ummoning positivity and affirmations to enlighten or shine a light on your *internal and external limiters*.

Once you have completed the exercise, review it and take yourself back into that situation and re-think how or what you could have done differently. Your next step in restoration is to research ways to untwist these cognitive distortions. Untwisting and retooling yourself to be able to DIGS disempowering, limiting beliefs, incongruences, Cognitive Dissonance and Distortions will allow you to live your life more freely, with more meaning and positively. Watch your abilities, skills and knowledge skyrocket in your 7 life areas. Do it for you. Do it for your family. Do it now.

Chapter 5
E + R = O
Timorous

"A man becomes what he thinks about most of the time."
Ralph Waldo Emerson

"The power plant does not have energy, it generates energy." Brendon Burchard

<u>Timorous</u>: characterized by or indicating fear; filled with fear

When you were worried about a situation you generated feelings. Did your emotional response cure or intensify the belief, feelings or actions? Your responses to an event will absolutely impact the outcome. E + R = O. Events +

Response = Outcome. You can choose how you will respond. Understanding both emotional conscious and subconscious responses is about taking the time to learn how you handle certain, common situations.

Exercise #5: Write down one example of how you responded to something recently, in each of your 7 life areas. If you can think of more, absolutely, write them down. You will gain more by acting, doing or practicing than by thinking or wishing. Likewise, you will learn and grow by completing these exercises, and in how seriously you take them. To grow, two things must happen, "Either something new comes to you or something comes from within you." Brendon Burchard

You must be willing to look back in your life to break down prior actions/reactions to understand how you can improve or respond more healthily moving forward and becoming and living your highest self.

Unfortunately, most of our responses are subconscious, we just react. When someone scares you, you instantly react by either jumping, screaming, hitting or taking a defensive stance. You did not take the time to think about it, you just responded. Reactive versus Proactive. The difference lies within your upbringing and training thus far in life. You can always be startled or scared, but your auto-response can be fine-tuned to a more desirable or palpable response.

Over your lifetime, either through lessons, actions or beliefs, you adopted a timorous mentality. You generated a self-confidence shell made purely of fear, worry and angst.

Why do timorous people tend to fail?

1. The timorous avoid failure by justifying through reasons, excuses and answers.
2. The timorous are ashamed and disgraced of failing.
3. The timorous are disappointed and discouraged by failing.

4. The timorous panic when confronted with a failure experience.
5. The timorous fear failure and give up easily when faced with failing.
6. The timorous avoid success opportunities or discredit them.
7. The timorous allow limiting beliefs of fears to have absolute control their lives.
8. The timorous live and believe in, without question, cognitive distortions.
9. The timorous do not seek help.
10. The timorous do not exercise to grow their mind, body and souls
11. The timorous do not question their auto-responses, in fear of failing when trying anew.
12. The timorous live in fear and are afraid to admit it.
13. The timorous exists in 93% of you.

What else could be said of timorous people? Whether it is the fear of failure or success or a combination of the two, limiting beliefs and actions of being a shy person keeps you living a caged or controlled life. You tend not to push boundaries, ask questions or go the extra mile. You are caged in the sense that you do not want to upset anyone, in fear of embarrassment or "failure" of being labeled as disrespectful or "one of those people" or for whatever reason. Abandon it. Now.

Here are some more examples of auto-responses. From cowering to bursting into an irrational emotional or vocal response: laughter, crying, anger or surprise. Scientist are trying to figure out how and why people fly into moments of rage. In 2015, a 30-year-old mother was arrested and charged with suddenly attacking her child's second grade teacher. During a road rage incident in Sacramento, California, Donald Bell received his moments of infamy by shooting and killing another motorist, Timothy Mann. Then just a few weeks later, Bell committed suicide. Why do we allow our auto-responses to be negative? Imagine if only

50% more of us decide to take ownership and upend our negativity, how would this impact you, your community, your state, your Country, our World?

These moments of rage can be harnessed and used as it is intended too. In 2009, Jasper Schuringa said "I didn't think," as he dove over several rows of seats to subdue a terrorist trying to set off a bomb on Northwest Flight 253. Again, your body is an incredible tool or instrument and is your most expensive, prized possession. Protect it. Nourish it. Challenge it. Use it.

The subconscious fools you every day. For example, when you eat. You know how a hamburger or a salad tastes. You automatically consume these types of foods without even consciously tasting it. You eat to fill the engine, not your taste buds. Scientists and experts have theorized that your brain automatically knows how a certain item(s) will taste before you take a bite. Try this the next time your bite into a burger, fish, bread or salad. Taste it. Savor it. Tastes do change. Tastes change every few years. Don't limit healthier eating by remembering how something used to taste. Try it. You may now like it. Novelty is another rewarded action.

You have heard and probably have even said the following, "*Sticks and stones may break my bones, but names or words will never hurt me.*" Nonsense. Broken bones heal. Bruises restore. Egos, not so easily. Disempowering beliefs, maybe not ever. Your words that you choose to use in communications with your children, family, friends or complete strangers do have a weighty impact. Has anyone ever told you, "You aren't good enough to do that."? How did it make you feel? Did you ever forget about the person that said this or something like this to you? If asked, could you recall the conversation as though it happened moments ago? Exactly. Disempowering beliefs start with the words you choose to use. Remember this when you are a parent, grandparent, coach, teacher, mentor, sibling, whichever. Names and words are more powerful than any stick or stone.

As soon as you say something and you regret saying it. Catch yourself and apologize, emphatically and immediately. Imagine the impact of what you are saying might have on the other person. Think bigger than yourself. Is there something better or another way to say what you are trying to say without generating emotional and disempowering beliefs? It is best to stay positive. Everyone wants to go negative, it is a poison, an infectious affliction that catches like a wildfire. Think about it. When you are around a group of "friends" and the conversation is negatively imbalanced, how does this make you feel? It truly is the proverbial pebble and pond. The ripples grow far and wide.

You will slip up and say something hurtful. Don't let it "lay out there to sink in" so that you cut deep and generate painful feelings in another person. Take control of your emotions and show some restraint. After counting to 10, 20, or even 100, if it will change the situation for the betterment, then go for it. Otherwise, if it will not change what has been done thus far, stop it with you. Be the bigger person and stop. "It takes a bigger person to walk away than to stand and argue." Be bigger. Be bolder. Be a positive influence.

If after the air has been cleared and you still have some emotional turmoil, go chop some wood or go for a long walk, bike ride, jog, drive, swim or sit in a classroom of silence. Close your eyes and say to yourself, "When I open my eyes, I will be at a level 10, filled with vibrancy and gratitude and the highest version of myself. Go ahead. Try it now. Just by choosing the words vibrant and gratitude gives you energy. See, your words are very powerful. There are tens of thousands of words that are positive. Start today. Start each day with a positive call.

Is there someone that you need to call to forgive, let go and begin healing right now? Just a quick call to an old friend or acquaintance that the two of you, parted ways in choppy seas, to say, "I am not asking you for anything in return, I just wanted to call and say how sorry I am for having left things the way I did. Will you forgive me? If not, I understand, but I wanted to clear my conscious so that I can go on living life to my fullest and highest self. Good-bye." Then disconnect the call. If they want to add anything, they can call you, if not, consider it closed. It takes a bigger person to call and apologize first. Do it now. Call and forgive somebody right now. Then continue to read, learn and grow. Good luck.

Like the words you generate in conversations, you generate your emotions too. Be boldly mature in how you respond the next time something happens. Look over your list of items that you wrote down in your 7 life-areas. How could you have changed your reaction so that it was positive to that same situation? Go ahead and list 1-3 positive alternatives to how you could have responded differently.

By living mindfully present and treasuring the moment, you soon realize how robotic your responses have been. It isn't who you are now, nor someone you wanted or dreamt of being, or anyone you would want to spend any amount of time getting to know. You allow yourself to get lost in the busyness of your work. Just as the body rebuilds in 7 years, choose which emotion or response you will re-generate, not in years, but literally in milliseconds. Choose, decide and act to be your highest self always. Be courageous.

To change, you must consciously generate the appropriate emotions. To change, you need to look inside of your heart and soul, through deep examination, meditation or prayer; commit to continuous learning and conscious re-training of your old habits (re-branding who you are now) and lastly, by taking necessary steps to change your responses to all events. This will bring about new, positively charged outcomes that you control. Today, if "X" happens, how do you respond? Differently or more of the same? My point, please don't allow the dream killers to pass on their trash (limiting beliefs). Say to yourself, what Jack Canfield trains his audiences, "No matter what you say or do to me, I am still a worthwhile and loveable person." "Sticks and stones may break my bones, but my thoughts are so much more powerful to me."

Stop being timid and tender. It is not you, anymore. Be a dreamer again.

Chapter 6
Mediocrity and its ugly cousins.
"We are, our worst enemy."

<u>Mediocrity</u>: Of only ordinary or moderate quality; neither good nor bad; barely adequate.

<u>Minimalistic Performer</u>: A person who favors a moderate approach to the achievement of a set of goals or who holds minimal expectations for the success of a program, relationship or job.

<u>Relativism</u>: Any theory holding that criteria of judgment are relative, holding that truth, moral or aesthetic value is not universal or absolute, *varying with individuals and their environments*.

Mediocrity is killing your Country and World. Mediocrity has become commonplace in your life. Like negativity, mediocrity is as infectious as it comes.

If two people are working, one giving it 100% and the other doing the very least to stay employed, what process exists in your organization or company to reward the higher performer? Do you have anything to recognize the extraordinaire? If I were to parachute into your past, how would I see you and your efforts 6 months ago? Would you be giving it your best, 100% of the time, or would you be doing as little as possible just to stay employed and getting paid?

Is it easy to give 100% in an organization, company or corporation that rewards mediocrity for a false sense of accomplishment; where everyone gets recognized for just showing up and paid the same? If your current employment, class or circle of influence is not challenging you to perform or be at your highest and best self, then why in the hell are you still there, participating in a defeatist atmosphere? You have become complacent and mediocre. Truth hurts. Truth stings. Truth creates hunger. Hunger generates inspiring and bold action. The hungrier you are, the more impact you will impart.

Challenge yourself to either generate positive and productive change in your current place of employment or spend your nights and weekends seeking a more conducive and positive position either in your current company or career field. If you cannot find one, maybe it is time to start your own. Reward based on performance, not fairness. Life is not fair. Admit it. Be the precipitator of positive change. I am not saying to go bust down walls, but to choose your words and actions carefully, to drop challenges amongst your co-workers and colleagues. Don't walk on egg shells. Speak softly and carry a big stick. The big stick is your attitude. Be positive. Be uplifting. Give credit where it is due.

The time is now to challenge you, your team and your management to be #1 in your industry. Rather than asking how, ask what it would take to be #1. How and where would you start? You must begin now, before comfort, complacency and mediocrity sets in at a potentially "higher" level, but still not at your team's best. The universe rewards action. The universe rewards positivity with positivity. The universe rewards you for being your highest self.

Minimalistic behaviors are an increasing and penetrating plague. Another ugly step cousin is relativism, whereas each person uses their own criterion and live by their own set of rules. You decide that current societal and practiced rules and or laws ought to be interpreted independently for you. Rid yourself of "friends" or circles of influence that are full of relativism-type people. You owe it to yourself. Find a mentor. Find a person of influence and ask them to coach you once a week or month. Find and create a new high performing people of influence group. It will make your life that much more interesting and less stressful.

Mediocrity, minimalism and relativism all combined is an absolute recipe for disaster. These tolerated behaviors will sink the largest, sturdiest ships, the most successful of businesses and even end the best campaigns while it continues to create a culture of negativity and resentment. These behaviors are running amuck and commonly without challenge within all societies, groups, organizations, corporations and governments right now. To simplify:
Good equals dead.
Great equals mediocre.
Excellent equals notice.
Extraordinaire equals triumph.
Imagine life as a slope, either you are challenging, educating or growing (moving upwards) or you are slipping (sliding backwards) and dying. There is no more "standing or sitting still" (complacency). Not for you who are reading this book and implementing the success principles shared. You have and will do it again, throw life in cruise control. Again, the purpose of this book is to D.I.G.S. your entire life. This book serves as an incredible tool to keep reading and implementing. If you think about it, the potential in any career is infinite. If you were to try 5% harder each time you read this book, there is no cap, no end to your potential and possibility. It is truly infinite.

When you "throw it in cruise," you will be passed and not because your cruise control wasn't properly working or failed to keep you moving. You jumped into the passenger seat of life. Face it, you became complacent, lazy and in due course, mediocre once again. Remember, life is a slope. There is no more parking or cruising allowed. The closer to the top you get, the steeper the climb. Embrace it. Enjoy it. Encompass its challenges.

Will you have days that you are "off" and not at your highest self? Sure. Will everyday be rosier and challenge free?" No. I mean, can you be flexible in successfully maneuvering the hardships, but resilient enough to stay on track, focused and pursuing your dreams and goals? Absolutely.

Imagine the difference you will make when you spawn a *5% more* culture. Challenging everyone to give just 5% more effort. No matter the size of your team, it quickly becomes infinite in its potential, possibility and pursuit. Hang on, and watch your team grow, enjoy and look forward to coming to work, again. Imagine the discussions around the water cooler. Imagine the productivity on the floor. Imagine the psychology of positivity that you created. Dare to dream. Dare to imagine. Dare to pay it forward.

I know that you have heard and even used the saying, "to give 110%". Don't use it. You cannot give more than 100%, period. I understand that it may be humanity's way of saying to not hold anything back from doing your best. Just ask for their best, 100% of the time. Release the brakes and thrust life's gas pedal to the floor, you will quickly set yourself apart from the rest.

Quoting John Paul Getty, a self-made billionaire, "Try harder." Try harder to do more this moment than the last. Try harder on this project than you did on the last. Try harder to learn more today than you did yesterday. Try harder on this test than the prior test. Try harder in this inning, quarter or half than the last. Try harder this anniversary than the last. Try harder on opening your mind and heart to learn and love more than ever before. Try harder spiritually. Try harder to stick with a healthier lifestyle. Try harder to discover, realize and visualize what you want your legacy to be when the time comes. Try harder, you cannot fail. Learn to "fail-forward", learning more this time than the last. Without fear, there cannot be courage.

Try harder in every area of your life, and watch your abundance grow. Your potential is without limits, it truly is infinite. Just by trying harder, you will not know how far you will go. Go blindly where no one has gone before. Try harder to fail forward. Without failure, success doesn't happen or exist.

Speaking of trying harder, let's shift gear to the limitless environment you live in today. It is unbelievably interesting. It is so incredibly fast paced. It is so ever changing. Imagine if former Apple CEO and Founder Steve Jobs didn't try harder to get a computer into every household. Where would Apple be without Jobs' try harder attitude? Would you be listening to music, wirelessly and remotely? Would smartphones exist? I am not saying that someone else may not have gotten us to this point, but who will lead us to the next level, whatever it may be?

Again, it is difficult to see into the future without looking to where you have been. Celebrate successes and failures along the way. Trying harder has opened so many new ideas and inventions.

All it took was for one civilian, with a lot of money, to launch his own company to put a private rocket into space, one man created the company, his team created the rocket. People are now free diving hundreds of feet, running a 4-minute mile or a remarkable 4.2 – 40-yard dash and you have even witnessed the fastest man on earth, Usain Bold, running 27.78 miles per hour! All examples of differently focused people living to their fullest potential, trying harder and refusing to settle.

You live in an instant gratification world, no doubt. However, those that are setting records are delaying their gratification, until after their goal is accomplished. None of this would be possible, unless that somebody was bold and brave enough to do it, first. Success leaves clues. Much was not possible until one person achieved it, and shared their story. Then it inspired others, maybe you. You will gravitate to those who are interesting and inspiring. Choose wisely. "Birds of a feather, flock together." "You will become who and what you think and act like every day." "Make your influencers the right ones."

As I have shared before, mediocrity, minimalism and relativism have infected all areas of society. There are 7% of people that are not like this, they resist the allure and temptation of ease or the comfortable life. They are what I classify as "*people of possibility (or influence)*". This group never settles or accepts the norm or become complacent in their views. These influencers are always pushing for excellence and improvements in all areas of their life. You might say that if you continually "try harder" that you will run out of things to say, do, pursue or ways to surprise. That's the beauty within it. As you make trying harder a habit, then layers get exposed, some things become easier to accomplish, and as you continue to try 5% more even after those things become easier then you are truly becoming a student of excellence – even extraordinaire.

Challenge #3: Surround yourself with "people of possibility". Those who are shooting for excellence, not existence, as they convey and create a positive, engaging, challenging and extraordinaire mentality. Ask. Ask. Ask. These "people of possibility" are willing to share their success and vision. It is captivating and a unique gravitational pull for you to become a part. Start building your own Dream Team.

Consider yourself "under construction" by being a true and practicing "student of excellence." No matter what you may call it, you become what you think about and act incessantly.

Build synergy with these dream makers. Set up a local Extraordinaire Cluster. Come together weekly or bi-monthly, if the Cluster is building synergy and enthusiasm, allow this to be your guide to meeting frequency. Allow each person an allotted amount of time to share. Understanding that if it is something very new, intriguing or of genuine interest to the Cluster, allow that person a little extra time. The key is to make sure the Cluster is being helpful to each participant and building synergy in your community or expertise.

Synergy is the interaction of elements that when combined, produce a total effect that is greater than the sum of the individuals and contributions. Build a boardroom filled with students of excellence. Build a synergetic and vibrant team. Be bold and flexible. Avoid being timid and tender. Be bold in your life. If it is to be, it is up to me!

Exercise #6: Part 1: Write down at least one person in each life-area that you admire, respect or want to emulate. Part 2: Rate yourself. On a scale of 1 to 10, 1 being dismal and 10 being vibrant and exciting, rate each of your areas. No more excuses, take "baby steps". You need to start someplace, be it a rating of 3 or 7, we can all be, do, give and try harder.

Part 3: Review your score. Take the areas that you are not at a level 10, and ask, "What must change within me to make it a 10?" Do it now.

Finances/Professional, Education/Self Improvement, Recreation/Hobbies, Health/Body/Fitness, Relationships/Family, Personal/Spiritual and Contributions/Legacy.

Life is too short, not to share your learnings, insights and gifts. You fail to be explicit with people. Explicit means clearly expressed, developed, formulated or demonstrated. Don't be rude. Praise in public and coach in private.

Granted, there are some people that are trying to impose advice all the time. It's about balance, tact and professionalism. When you receive excellent service, you may financially compensate a professional. Beyond financially, how else could you compensate them? Be extraordinaire. Extraordinaire in your delivery and advice is not the norm. You will be remembered.

Whether it is while dining, shopping, driving, conversing, working or attending a spiritual or inspirational event, be extraordinaire, defining who you are now and not how you were categorized.
Forever trying harder each moment. Forever pushing for excellence. Forever refining and improving processes. Do this in all 7 areas of your life. Who are you now? Who are you going to be?

Exercise #7. You just evaluated yourself, now write 2-3 goals in the 7 life-areas starting by thinking, acting and speaking about who you will become in "X" months. When setting these goals, set rigid checkpoints, benchmarks and milestones. Details with completion days and times.

Statistics and studies have shown that only 3% of society has active, written goals. Ironically, 97% work for these 3%! Once written, share these with your spouse, family, mentor, coach, and friends, Priest or Spiritual Advisor. This is the new you!

Chapter 7
Conscious - Sub Conscious
"Life is found in the dance between your deepest desire and greatest fear." Anthony Robbins

The conscious mind (brain) can be exposed and studied, the incredible structures are nearly indescribable but basically, the brain's functions are studied and are well known. It is where you consciously think and live.

The sub-conscious mind (mind) operates regardless to your conscious thought or control. It operates 24 hours a day, throughout your entire lifetime and directs all of your bodily functions such as breathing, heart beating and digestion, in short everything that allows you to live. Imagine if you had to consciously decide to breath, have your heart beat at the perfect timing, blood flow levels and pressures throughout vessels, arteries and appendages, as well as chewing gum and walking. You could not consciously do all of this, you just would not last 60 seconds. We have literally trillions of sensory pulses firing simultaneously, to keep you alive and active. This all "just happens" without us knowing. Welcome to your subconscious mind.

The Infinite mind is where depth and knowledge is generated. I understand and respect that you may or may not agree with this, but for the sake of argument, let's call it that place where you come up with all of your ideas and actions. Rest assured, there are no limits to what you can imagine and do if you follow 5 steps: 1. Identify 2. Clarify 3. Listen for giving Purpose. 4. Believe with all of heart and soul. 5. Affirm your belief tens of times per day or at a minimum, when you first wake and last thing before you fall to sleep and during any breaks you take. The Infinite Mind contains all knowledge and power: past, present & future.

There is so much information about the brain, both conscious and unconscious (sub-conscious). I am not a scientist, but a guy with a vision (dream), passion and intense belief to help others like you overcome disempowering, limiting beliefs and mediocrity. Scientists know that we use (at minimum) these four lobes of the brain, in which the first <u>three</u> are used for thoughts and actions.

Frontal Lobe
Parietal Lobe
Temporal Lobe
Occipital Lobe

Frontal Lobe's functions range from behaviors and personality to judgement and mood. Parietal Lobe's functions range from intelligence to language and reasoning to reading. The Temporal Lobe's functions range from speech to emotions and memory to hearing and vision. While the Occipital Lobe handles only vision. This is your "projection" room. Life is a series of motion pictures. This is why you must have reminders, positive quotations and visualizations that surround you. Replay these affirmations in your mental movie theater.

"Watch your thoughts, for they become words. Choose your words, for they become actions. Understand your actions, for they become habits. Study your habits, for they will become your character. Develop your character, for it becomes your destiny." Unknown

Each of us are born with a special "Gift" or human version of a GPS system to guide us. It is when you are "off course" that you experience the lack of congruency or cognitive dissonance. When your actions do not align with your beliefs and values, you may feel anxiety, a knotting feeling in your stomach, an outburst of anger, fear, disappointment or mental fatigue, as your brain has structural tension, pumping endorphins into your system to "right the wrong". These endorphins give us super human strength when necessary. Your upbringing has such a powerful impact on how you process things well into your 20s. Particularly important in your developmental years are the words and phrases that you hear or those that are directed at you. While parents, teachers and coaches are still human, most do not realize the power their words carry. Be careful in how you speak to anyone, but especially, the young and impressionable. This goes both ways. This is the delicate dance between instilling values and generating fears, beliefs, inconsistencies and cognitive distortions. Your words, tone and delivery are key.

Don't limit thinking, believing or dreaming. Embrace it. You do not know who will come up with the next invention or technologically advancing tool. Seek to empower others to help bring out their special gift, as it already exists and just needs to be brought to the conscious mind or surface. Everything already *exists* within someone's infinite mind. Having both the willingness and courage to bring forth your gift or idea from your infinite mind into your conscious mind and then to act with this idea, dream or passion. Your gift may be new in the sense that it is the first time anyone has heard it aloud, but, was it truly "new"?

This movement is about creating and generating inspiration to share your gifts. Therefore, we need to create positive cultures inside and outside of our classrooms, offices, churches and homes. It is about pushing limits, not arguing societal norms. Debating is healthy and constructive, arguments are not.

Arguments often generate maladaptive behaviors, attitudes and perceptions. Arguments breed perpetuating hostility and potential life-long lasting resentment and *loss*. The *loss* of focus on many other, much more important issues that need to be resolved.

Our time would be better spent by tapping into your infinite mind. You will be better understood and respected when you acknowledge and admit to the other person's viewpoint.

Exercise #8: Sit in a room of silence, pick a product, service or relationship. Tap into your Infinite Mind and see how you could improve it immediately in your life. Maybe you have been living in the *busyness of life* and not *your purposeful life*. If you learn nothing from this book but only this observation, then it was worth its weight in gold. "Most people do not listen with the intent to understand. They listen with the intent to reply." SLOW down time. Listen. Understand. Encourage.

Exercise #9: Take some time right now to pick one life-area (not like the prior exercise) that you want to see grow the most. Forget about who you were yesterday or the moment prior to this chapter. Expand on your definition of who you will be going forward from this exact point now. Who will you be in 1 – 3 – 5 – 10 – 20 years?

<u>Write this down</u>!

Visualize with such intensity, belief, gratitude and genuineness and watch your life's riches grow.

"The universe rewards action."

Chapter 8
Mindfulness: Quiet Mind

Mindfulness: A technique in which one focuses full attention only in the present, experiencing thoughts, feelings and sensations and not judging them.

Quiet Mind: A quiet mind is one with no thoughts, only darkness. Some say it is impossible to reach this state of mind, and maybe it is, but, for the sake of learning, please appease me for a chapter or two.

Meditation: Continued or extended thought; reflection; contemplation. Devout religious contemplation or spiritual introspection.

Mindfulness is practicing an action while you are awake and immersed in life. Meditation is typically done in a closed environment, away from the busyness of life. Either way, mindfulness or showing genuine appreciation and gratitude, has been proven to reduce stress and even real, physical pain. Many of the world's top advisors meditate. Many of the top inspirational and motivational people practice mindfulness (and meditate). Be mindful of your surroundings, acknowledge and be gracious that you may have the freedom and abilities to entirely appreciate what has been created.

You may suffer from chronic pain and use mindfulness, meditation and visualizations to cope. A movement that would be accepted, especially in many US Veterans Administration hospitals and clinics, is what I would call "meditation over medication." In short, Mind over Matter.

I write to you with a grateful and thankful heart that I learned at an early age, the damage addictions can wreak on one's belief system and self-esteem. I know that addictions are real. I know that addictions are not given the appropriate amount of attention. You may know someone suffering from an addiction. Tap into your infinite mind and seek alternative solutions; you must seek "meditation over medication" (literally or figuratively).

You must be committed to constant and never ending improvement. You must acquire a desire to live a mindful and purposeful life. Throughout my years, I have learned more about myself through study and prayer and have realized that "if it is to be, it is up to me."

Brendon Burchard often states that only two things can happen: 1. Something new comes into your life. 2. Something new comes from within you. Most likely, something new must come from within you.

By practicing mindfulness, you will be amazed on how you can improve on so many more things in life. Be courageous and bold enough to share your ideas. And remember: No more excuses, reasons, answers or self-justifications.

It is up to you, if you keep an open heart, mind and soul. Possess the boldness and courage to do whatever it takes to fulfill a desire or calling. As you are aware, it is not easy to "follow your heart." You will meet even more trials (mediocre people) in all walks of life. No matter their circumstances or situation, they choose to just exist, to be a follower. Within a few seconds, you realize if a person is an influencer or a dream killer.

All living things put out an energy pulse or aura. Be fully present, attune to this person, providing undivided attention and practice listening with the intent to understand, not with the intent to reply. Ask questions. Ask people why they do what they do. Become inquisitive and intriguing. As many, much wiser than I have said, there are two types of people in this world, sheep and wolves. Which are you? Which do you feed, continually, consciously and subconsciously? Can you switch between the two based on circumstances? Answer this, if you are a wolf, charging forward in your life, with genuine authenticity and gratitude, how can you become a sheep? There is nothing wrong with being a sheep, if that's the life you want to live and accept. If so, you have accepted and planted a limiting belief somewhere along the line.

However, if you are reading this book and completing the exercises, you are not a sheep. You are a wolf. If you are reading this book and not doing the exercises, you will be a wealth of shelf knowledge. Shelf knowledge: To know and not do, is not yet to know. Chew on that. Bahhhh-Bahhhh.

A quiet mind is the only way to declutter and manage life. With a quiet mind, you are more likely to respond as your highest self and not as a hyper-maniac. A maniac where anger blazes, temper flares and inflammatory emotions threaten to burn part of your life to ashes. A quiet mind is the only way to solve your problems calmly, intelligently and logically. A quiet mind is the only way to maintain mental command over problem-people – no matter how insulting, no matter how arrogant, and no matter how hostile they are.

We take in so much information and it seems to never end. Slow down time. Strive for a quiet mind. Stay positive. Use all your brain's lobes to their limitless potential. Don't wait for a dramatic event to slow down time. Have you ever experience slow time? Ask anyone who was in a very serious accident, incident or war. It truly is amazing the details your brain can process, yet it seems everything is in slow motion.

Speaking of limitless. Your memory is astonishing too. You may not know or realize it, but your memory is attached to all your senses. It remembers how something should look, taste, smell and feel. It even knows how a particular food should taste. Taste, no, really _taste_ your food. In such a hectic, fast paced life, you are involuntary rushed to eat, if get to a chance to eat at all. However, if you were to slow down time and be fully present, taking the time to enjoy the smell, taste and even feel the texture and delight to the palate, you would consume less food by filling more quickly. Hell of a great diet plan.

Your brain has no limits, but your conscious mind cannot maintain two active thoughts at the same time. Rather, you experience a cognitive dissonance of sorts.
Have you ever been to a nice restaurant where the waiter pours a small amount of wine into your glass, then you swirl the wine to look, smell it and then taste it? This is being fully aware and present, nothing else is on your mind, but truly savoring the flavor. Now you know why you need to sip wine and other beverages. Take full pleasure in the moment.

Challenge #4: During your next meal, take a small bite, close your eyes and chew slowly, try to guess the spices present, the texture, the smell, do they coincide with what you remember or is it a new recipe? When you are fully present, your food's taste will seem to have changed. Try this with a carbonated drink, take a sip and let it sit in your mouth a few seconds…. does it taste the same or can you taste the aluminum, the sweeteners, the carbonation bouncing off the tongue and roof of your mouth?

As I stated earlier, I am a "student of excellence" always challenging and learning as I grow. Life is a slippery slope, you must learn to savor life. Life is a marathon, not a sprint.

** I am neither a dietician nor doctor or anyone that offers paid advice on weight loss, so, please do not try this without first talking with your medical provider or professional advisor. While this has worked for millions, each person and case is unique to these results. **

In the United States, we are in a serious obesity epidemic. It is especially alarming in children. Experts have claimed and statistics support the conclusion that the millennial and Z generations could be the first generation to die before their parents. As a parent, you never want to outlive your children. Not only is obesity an epidemic, so are the number of diabetes and other medical cases, especially in children, becoming even more prevalent. Good news, in most cases, not all, type II diabetes and other medical cases are physically correctable and preventable if you are committed to making it so and without using medications.

It will and does take solid education, self-discipline, self-awareness and self-determination. This applies to absolutely everyone, no matter your age, circumstances or competencies. Wake up America! (Another epidemic, sleep deprivation!)

Chapter 9
Clarity and Consistency

How are you minimizing your life's red lights by green lighting the truest you?

Do you have written goals? Do you look at them regularly or do you even know where you left them? Have you sat in silence to find clarity; on a consistent basis? Are you comfortable in being confined, complacent and content?

What is stopping you from being a *Person of Possibility*, living an incredible, meaningful life? You know the answers already. You hold the answers within your beliefs, limited and safe.

It is common for you to seek approval for your actions. As children, you longed for the affirmations of your parents. As you grew older, you began to value the opinions of your friends, colleagues and employers. At times, the agendas of others created prerogatives with imposed authority or importance that they overshadowed yours and you lost sight of who you are. This prerogative now becomes their way to measure you and your worth as a person. Again, BS.

The world is becoming even more comforting to our misgivings, mishaps and mistakes. Truest dream killers. You must take the necessary time, daily, to find a way to clear your head, find clarity and reaffirm your goals on a scheduled and consistent basis. I know when I do not take the proper amount of time to mentally prepare for the day. Before I know it, it is noon and I have accomplished little towards my goals. You should feel awkward if you miss your time too.

Probe for the difficult questions: Why, When, Where, What, Who, How. You are smart. You know what to ask, be explicit and ask. 4-year olds are relentless when it comes to asking, "Why?"

You must dig deep, muster the courage and be boldly confident and ask. Quit accepting established disempowering or limiting beliefs. Think like your geometry teacher, deciding which "proof" you would use. Agendas of others teach you how you are supposed to respond. Break the mold.

Don't avoid being honest and genuine with people. Quit sweeping misgivings and false beliefs under the proverbial rug. Quit reasoning in your head. Reasoning ranging from having lived a difficult life to being raised within a dysfunctional family to being a victim of a wrecked system and nearly destroyed environment. So many damn excuses, reasons or answers.

There were, are and will be more challenges that lay before you. Stand with boldness, clarity and consistency. Consistently preparing, as often as necessary, to maintain and strengthen your choices, goals and dreams; and with absolute and unwavering purity and definitive action.

Ask more pertinent, intelligent questions, and often. You are inspired by some and turned off by others. Why? Whose opinion matters most to you? Be the person you want to be. If you are reading this book, you are not a complacent or mediocre person. You are seeking ways and tools to help facilitate change. You have become dissatisfied with your assessment in the way you are living. You must quit living comfortably and offer more help to others. Want to join a positive, productive movement? Then read on!

Most people are afraid to ask. Ask to learn. Question experts, new and old, either through inner-views and research or through their books and blogs. People love to talk about themselves. Successful people want to pass along the secrets to their success. Seek. Discover. Share.

"Success leaves clues." Essentially, it all boils down to doing what others are not willing to do or put the time into accomplishing it. Call it comfort, complacency or mediocrity.

The system is failing all of us. Entitlement is not a right, but a privilege. When you decide to start asking the intelligent and challenging questions, the sooner you will depart with the sheep herd and be welcomed as a member of the *wolf* pack. Follow this one success principle: Ask, Ask, Ask.

You have, on average, 78 years of life to find your mission, purpose, and spirit or core genius. The earlier in life that you can find clarity amongst these, the more time you will live like the 7%. The earlier you will embrace a more fulfilling, happy, impactful and far reaching life.
I remind you again, no more excuses, reasons, answers or self-justifications. Find clarity. Be decisive. Start new habits. Dream Big. And set Goals.

"In the absence of clearly-defined goals, we become strangely loyal to performing daily trivia until ultimately we become enslaved by it." Robert Heinlein, American Novelist.

By expanding your horizons, setting your sights much further than you have ever imagined, you too can continue to D.I.G.S. and living a higher purposed life. Life's purpose, visions, missions, goals and dreams will become much clearer, much faster, with much more abundance.

Intense clarity coupled with self-disciplined consistency will stop you from limiting beliefs. Imagine when you have this clarity and consistency in each of the 7 life-areas. How peaceful would that be for you and your relationships?
The likelihood of these *dream killers* creating any cracks in your dreams crust is insignificant.

You will share new insights and gifts with the World and not just your existent, small circle of family and friends. Life is like the sea, it may be rough and turbulent on the surface, but deep within you, there exists a certain calmness, peace and inner beauty just waiting to shine. When you define the "why" in making this positive change, there will be nothing that can stop you. (Other than your worst enemy, your negative inner voice.)

The *why* is fundamental to unlocking life's greatest treasures. When you have a well thought-out, emotionally and physically charged answer behind your *why*; the more of life's abundance you will be rewarded. Far beyond petty, earthly material things, but through making a difference in the lives of millions. Dare to dream bigger. Dare to question. Dare to be bold. The world watched as a man walked on the moon in 1969, proving that the sky is infinite. So, there are no limits beyond those we either inherit or create.

Don't worry about *how*, but rather focus on where and who you want to be and become. "A *man* becomes what *he* thinks about most of the time." Ralph Waldo Emerson.

It is difficult to mine your deepest, darkest memories that you have so cleverly compartmentalized within your brain. Subconsciously, this could be the one key defining your current life and circumstances.

Find the "what" that's holding you back from living life freely, without regret, remorse or remiss. Stand strongly. Stand inquisitively. Stand confidently.

Victory in your *Journey* will require the use of neuroplasticity. Neuroplasticity, in short, is the capacity of the nervous system (brain) to develop new neural connections. In other words, you consciously redirect (creating new neural pathways) from your old habitual patterns of behavioral responses.

You become self-aware or even hyper-aware of disempowering or limiting beliefs and choose consciously how you deal with each. To change these auto-response behaviors, you must identify these moments and then create new pathways (responses/thoughts) to match your highest self or as I call it, the truest **you**.

I understand that we live in a very fast paced world, unarguably. Hence, many have not taken the time to mature emotionally. Emotional immaturity is something that we all can learn more about in subsequent books. I hope that I have poked a nerve, or piqued your interest enough to get your undivided attention, no matter your age or circumstances. While many say, anger clouts the mind; I say that with proper conscious, disciplined awareness training, you will create clarity within the clout, it is a matter of retraining your brain. E + R = O.

Chapter 10
Exercises to Learn, Love and Live

As I mentioned earlier, the purpose of Life's Stop Lights Series is based on a dream, passion and willingness to help you and millions of others. Either directly or indirectly; decide and ignite the fire in your belly to challenge yourself consistently, behaving as your highest self-100% of the time, Living life freely, mindfully and with gratitude.

You are no longer a sheep, following the herd or the masses. You are a wolf, that makes the sheep nervous. You have witnessed, maybe even practiced and allowed relativism to become commonplace. How is this working for your life, family, country or world? Is it better than how you found it? Why not try what you have learned thus far.

Chances are that you have, up to this point, lived in fear, resentment, regretfully, performing well below your potential and not fully present or your highest self.

Example: Physically, I was present as my kids grew. However, mentally I was not so much. I was enslaved by busyness that came with work. My heart became encrusted, I was no longer happy and was quite honestly, lost. To this day, there are a lot of "memories" that my family enjoy that I cannot recall. It is a standing joke when my family talks about these memories, and just say, "Never mind Dad, you were working with X."

I was utterly lost in the busy work and not my life's work. It may take a series of interventions to either knock you off your high horse or a medical emergency to wake you to be able to fully appreciate life, keeping your eyes, ears and heart open. Ultimately, you will find your truest self and giving-purpose when you look deep inside of your soul and ask a simple question: "Am I happy?" "Am I happy in all 7 life areas right now? Only you know.

As I pontificated earlier about communications and the importance of it, please allow me to share a life's lesson on living to our fullest potential. Hearing is the sense by which sound is perceived. Listening is giving attention with the ear, joining closely for hearing and understanding.

You hear and you may listen. It is not easy to be a good listener. It takes practice. You know when you have the other person's undivided attention; do you suppose they know too, when you are not fully present and listening? You don't like having to restate things over and over, so is frustrates you.

Practice what you preach. Actively listening is an art and takes consistent and conscious discipline to accomplish justly.

Commit to constant and never ending and attentive listening and watch your treasures grow.

Here are ten examples of Empowering Beliefs to practice:

1. The past does not equal the future.
2. There is always a way if I'm committed.
3. There are no failures, only outcomes – if I learn something I'm succeeding.
4. If I can't, I must; if I must, I can.
5. Everything happens for a reason and purpose that serves me.
6. I find great joy in little things…. a smile…a flower…. a sunset.
7. I give more of myself to others than anyone expects.
8. I create my own reality and am responsible for what I create.
9. If I'm confused, I'm about to learn something.

10. Every day above ground is an incredible day of opportunities.

As I have mentioned before, your memories are a series of motion pictures. You will remember faces but not names. You will remember the emotion you had during a conversation, but not all the details. You may be able to place somebody, but not know how, when or why. Be the active listener and you will prosper in a very self-centered, self-serving world. Be the extraordinaire you know you can be.

By listening and using associations with a person you just met as well as repeating their name 2-3 times during your conversation, you will never forget that person's name. Watch how this impacts their response the next time you see them and call them by name. It sounds like common sense, but it is not common practice. I love this exercise because of the responses you get. They are perplexed, to say it nicely.

An association is an idea, image, feeling or saying, suggested by or connected with something other than itself; an accompanying thought, emotion or the like. Example: you meet someone at a sporting event, nursery, winery, school, or office with the name, Jill. You might associate Jill with the children's rhyme of Jack and Jill along with where you saw them. Again, these associations are completely up to your infinite and creative minds and need to never be heard or whispered from your lips. This gives your imagination free reins.

There are a lot of principles in books, online and in life. In the Dale Carnegie Course, "How to win friends and influence people" you learn 21 principles. The sixth principle, "Remember, a person's name is to him or her, the sweetest and most important sound in any language."

Challenge #5: As you see, meet or greet people, how many of their names do you know or can remember? Set yourself apart from the rest. Learn all their names, as quickly as you can. Use their name in your greetings and farewells. If you do not remember their name, ask them courteously. Don't make up an excuse. Chances are very good that they do not remember yours either. Be honest. Be genuine. Be explicit. Life is far too short to be timorous.

Remember, the sweetest and most important sound in any language….

Recall how you feel when someone calls you by name: vital, respected, admired and valued. You feel great when someone remembers your name, now remember theirs.

Hold high convictions and refuse to accept what appears to be the norm in too many organizations and corporations. Don't allow your frustrations with mediocrity, minimalism, hedonism, disempowering or limiting beliefs drive you crazy. Create a "safe" phrase that will automatically put you into a peaceful state of mind.

For example, if you love to fish, you might say to yourself when you are ready to burst into a tirade, "Boat." Boat reminds you of the peace and tranquility you experience when you are just floating and bobbing in the water. What will be your safe word or phrase? Another trick when you are feeling anxious or stressed. Try to imagine how the carpet, floor, road or path might feel. Is it soft? Is it solid? Is it grooved? Is it worn? This works very well while driving in heavy traffic, to take your mind off the offensive drivers that seem to get your blood boiling.

Remember to be a student of excellence to your highest, best and truest abilities. Help people. Help all people. Help people get out of a rut or funk. Inner-view everyone and anyone. He who has the most toys doesn't win. He who has the most loving relationships in life, wins.

Remember to ask, ask, and ask. If you don't ask, you will not receive. Asking good, open-ended questions to find out who they are and who they see themselves today and in X years. What are their dreams, wishes, regrets and do they have any advice? Always finish each conversation by asking, "How can I help you?" This will leave an amazing impression and increase your credibility as a genuine, loving and caring person. What goes around; will come around again.

Watch their faces light up when you ask them what they wanted to be when they grew up. Let them talk. Ask good, intelligent questions. Be inquisitive. Be genuinely interested in them. Ask how they got into their line of work, whether it was their dream or not. Ask them why they didn't pursue their dream to be a X. Share your current dreams and ask them for advice on how you can deliver on your life's giving-purpose and mission. Find out "their secrets" to life.

Share. Sow the seeds of knowledge. You are now a part of a movement. A movement to re-ignite joyfulness and gratitude in the world. You are unique in that you are getting in at the beginning of this new, growing and powerful movement to bring happiness back as a priority, not just money and material things.

Take time in the classroom of silence, daily, to learn about who you are, where you are headed, and write out your "master-life plan". How does it look, feel, smell, or taste like when you accomplish your plan? Decide your successes in each of your 7 life areas. Practice self-discipline and set checkpoints, benchmarks and milestones. Celebrate all successes along the way. Don't wait until the end. Try harder to push yourself out of the comfortable life and into the charged life and become a person of possibilities.

Don't wait. You will know when you achieve "success". You will feel it in every vein, nerve, tendon and muscle in your body. You will achieve that sense of joyfulness, mindfulness and presence, again, like when you were younger. Live like the 7%. Remember that 93% of people are unhappy. What would have to change in my life, to get me to a level 10 in all 7 life areas?

You may have received sage advice or limiting beliefs from your parents, grandparents, mentors and relatives. You may have heard some even say, "If you find a career that you love to do, you will never work a day in your life." What are you willing to do to reach this level of happiness in your professional life? Remember, when you have the "why" behind what you want, along with passion, conviction and the ability to delay complete gratification, there is absolutely nothing on this earth that can stop you.

You are your biggest critic. Your inner voice must remain positive, through daily meditation, prayer, reflections and affirmations. When someone rains on your parade, remember that the sun will always shine after the rain. Don't believe the nay-sayers or the dream killers. It is easier to sit back and poke holes in someone's dream than it is to dream infinitely and without regrets. The world is full of these dream killers, about 93%. Be honest. Be bold. Be yourself.

While reading this book, you may have ridden a tough rollercoaster of emotions, bringing up events and situations whereas limiting beliefs have crushed your dreams or paralyzed you in acting. Revisit all your dreams and reaffirm the dreams that you are pursuing.

Exercise 10: "If money, benefits and expectations were all met, and you could do anything that you love doing so much, that you would do it for free, what would that be? Where? When? Why? What is stopping you from pursuing your dreams now? You had 1000 excuses, but now you know your "why" behind what you are doing. "Dream big, it's free."
Mom

Nearly all the people that I have had the blessing to inner-view, wish that they could hit a reset button and start over. Many will also purchase this book series and use these new insights and completed exercises to hit their reset button.

Many may not have the self-discipline to do such a thing. It is not easy or comfortable to go against the grain of normalcy. You only have two choices, *change* or *more of the same.*

Don't wait until tomorrow, next month or the start of a new year. Don't allow a paper calendar to decide when or who you are. (That is placing a disempowering belief upon yourself.) Quit it. Choose to begin right now. Choose to live vibrantly, confidently, lovingly and with a perpetual aura of joy, love, health and abundance.
Make a commitment and stick with it using your strong self-discipline and new found self-awareness to disempowering, limiting beliefs and cognitive distortions. You owe it to yourself, your friends, your loved ones, your neighbors, your community, your state, your Country, your World.

Exercise #11: Close your eyes and say to yourself, "When I open my eyes, I will be my highest self."

> "No matter how bad it is or how bad it gets, I am going to make it!" Les Brown

I have witnessed some damn smart doctors and even more doctors that were rushed, complacent or disempowering in their diagnosis. They came from both the private and governmental sectors, so as to address anyone that thinks I am critiquing one system over another. I accept full responsibility in all areas of my life. I have apologizing down to a science, as I am not perfect, nor do I claim to be or hold all the answers.

To be honest, if it weren't for my dislike and frustration with complacency, I am not sure I could be so positive, uplifting and encouraging to others in parallel situations. I know that everyone in a wheel chair will not walk again, however, who's to say that it could not be possible?

Exercise 12: *Imagine* you are driving/riding in your car, minding your own business, in your lane and at the maximum speed limit, when and suddenly, another vehicle nearly runs into your bumper, swerves to pass you while casting an unattractive grimace or menacing *"wave"* then they cut back, right in front of you, barely missing the front of your car.

What do you do? How do you respond? Now, honestly answer this: Did your response make it better or escalated? Again, be honest. Re-read the response again. Now, how will you respond to these types of actions?

There are going to be dream killers, naysayers and negative people in all areas of your life and career. This response, if used honestly and frequently, really takes the wind out of your harmful responses and tendencies. Are you really going to let somebody ruin your day? Are you going to allow them to deflate your "happiness" bubble of singing or jamming-out to music, because they are having a bad day?

Please create your own business or note card with those statements. Place it on the dashboard of your vehicle. Make extras, share and pay it forward. Road rage is a real killer.

Congratulations on completing book one of the Life's Stop Lights series! I know that you have learned much and are now able to utilize D.I.G.S. to overcome any obstacle, challenge or blockade. I know this may be very overwhelming. But if you "chunk it down" by re-reading each chapter and completing the exercises honestly, you will undoubtedly begin living a much unrestricted life, as the yoke you had on your shoulders will now be gone.

"Sometimes we have to stop doing what we want or what is comfortable, and we must do what is required of us to grow and serve at a higher level." Brendon Burchard

Impactful and appropriate quotes to closing book one of Life's Stop Lights:

"If you accept a limiting belief, then it will become a truth for you." Louise Hay

"If you don't set a baseline standard for what you'll accept in your life, you'll find it's easy to slip into behaviors and attitudes or a quality of life that's far below what you deserve. You need to set and live by these standards no matter what happens in your life." Anthony Robbins (Limiting beliefs)

"Optimism is essential to achievement and it is also the foundation of courage and true progress." Nicholas M. Butler, American Philosopher (Cognitive dissonance)

"The primary cause of unhappiness is never the situation, but your thoughts about it. Be aware of the thoughts you are thinking." Eckhart Tolle (Cognitive distortion)

"It is better to be WORLD-CLASS at a few things than MEDIOCRE at many things." Darren Hardy

"Years ago, I had realized I was blaming myself for it. People and doctors would tell me it wasn't my fault, but I couldn't "BELIEVE" it! Then I was talking to my friend Kieran and he explained to me in a way that I could PERCEIVE that I was not at fault. No one else could ever do that before, though many tried. Many, many people had tried to tell me it wasn't my fault, but I was convinced it was my fault because I was trying to cheer up my dad." Robert Anthony (Cognitive Distortion)

"Courage is the ability to have faith, persistence and strength in the face of fear, pain and stress." "Keep persisting toward you dreams. Just because. Be strong even when you have all the reason in the world to be small. Do this, just because we need you. The world needs more people with a courageous heart." Brendon Burchard (Limiting beliefs)

"You begin to fly when you let go of self-limiting beliefs and let your mind and aspirations to rise to greater things." Brian Tracy

"All it takes is one person in any generation to heal a family's limiting beliefs." Gregg Bradon

"Chronic self-doubt is a symptom of the core belief, "I'm not good enough." We adopt these types of limiting beliefs in response to our family and childhood experiences, and they become rooted in our subconscious – we have the ability to take action to override it." Lauren Mackler

"Become aware of your beliefs and automatic default settings. Bring them into your light of your present, adult knowledge. Gently acknowledge that they are what they are. Then they constitute what you've believed until now, and that you can transform them into beliefs that you can fully express who you really are. Without judgement, patiently begin working to change subconscious and limiting beliefs into true expressions of your authentic self." Sue Thoele

"One of the hardest expressions of self-assertiveness is challenging your limiting beliefs." Nathanial Branden

"One of the first things that I do with people is to help figure out what their limiting beliefs are and encourage them to question, "Well, do I really want to keep that one? Is it limiting me? Does it not fit me? Is it holding me back?" Deborah King

"All too often we are filled with negative and limiting beliefs. We're filled with doubt. We're filled with guilt or with a sense of unworthiness. We have a lot of assumptions about the way of the world that are actually wrong." Jack Canfield

"Sometimes people hold a core belief that is very strong. When they are presented with evidence that works against that belief, the new evidence cannot be accepted. It would create a feeling that is extremely uncomfortable, called cognitive dissonance. And because it
is so important to protect the core belief, they will rationalize, ignore and even deny anything that doesn't fit in with the core belief." Frantz Fanon

"Don't live an unexamined life." Matthew Kelly

"Be happy where you are. Be grateful for what you have. But never settle for where you are. Improve yourself until the day you die." Unknown

"We are all just walking each other home." Rumi

Closing

I share my story in hopes that it will inspire you to take bold action, to refuse to accept further disempowering and limiting beliefs, to dream big again and to know that you have no limits, your love has no limits and your legacy has no limits.

Don't be afraid. Don't live in fear. Don't limit yourself. Life has no limits.

You will find it very difficult at first to live your highest self always. You are not more disadvantaged than anyone else. You are not a failure. You are not destined to live a life of complacency, mediocrity or hedonism. You are not at a point of no return. You were made for an extraordinaire purpose.

You are where you are, at the perfect time. You are reading this book and learning at the perfect time. You are now at the perfect time in your life to apply the foretold principles and challenges. You are open minded and coachable. You know that you *generate* all your feelings. You control who you are, want to be and where you are going. You will become hyper-aware of the many pitfalls and potential areas of painful and lasting harm.

You must now set goals for yourself and must be explicitly honest and transparent with yourself. Let your light shine. Embrace to understand who you are and what makes you happiest. Dreaming big takes the same amount of energy as dreaming shortsightedly.

You have no limits. You have infinite potential. Set your new goals based on this belief of no limits. Don't worry about the "how" in achieving your goals. Believe in yourself. Achieve extraordinaire.

D.I.G.S. **D**ecide your goal. **I**dentify your checkpoints, benchmarks and milestones. (Celebrate successes!) **G**enerate an action plan. Act as it your goal is accomplished. (How does it look? How does the air smell and taste? What are others saying about your achievement? How do you feel? Did you give 100%? Can you continue to try harder, push for even greater results?) **S**ummon positive affirmations and recall these at least 3 times a day, first thing upon waking, while you are taking a break and the last thing you do before you fall to sleep. D.I.G.S. works for everything.

Embrace it. Use it. Share it. You are now a part of a movement much larger than you. You are dared to help transform the world. You are a leader, coach and positive influence. You will be bold and go forth to live your highest self, always.

Journal and review your successes. Seek your next challenge with the tools you have been introduced or reintroduced to thus far. Begin to recognize how many disempowering, limiting beliefs you hear in a conversation.

Recognize the different cognitive distortions in those you interact. Begin to understand the feelings that you are consciously and subconsciously generating, i.e. anxiety,

angst, sleeplessness behaviors, worry, fear, anger, resentment. Embrace a positive alternative response or auto response system.
Tap into your infinite mind to find solutions to reach and realize your biggest dreams, childhood, adulthood, private or public. The how will just appear or come to you when the time is perfect, no matter what you are doing.

Practice and implement what you have read. Don't practice shelf-esteem. Shelf-esteem: to know and not do; is not yet to know. There are far too many "arm chaired cowboys" in your life already.

As you begin to achieve success, celebrate and share your successes. It is not bragging if you are celebrating your success with others. Life is a celebration, don't let anyone rain on your success parade.

If you have any suggestions or want to share your successes with the Author, please go to www.mcginnisconsultinggroup.com or email smileymcginnis@gmail.com. I want to hear about your struggles, accomplishments, lessons, questions and advice. As I have shared before, I too am a student of excellence as I am and will forever be, under construction. While I do not claim to be a doctor or therapist, I am genuinely interested in helping people from all walks of life. I am truly just a guy that refuses to accept societal, egotistical and disempowering beliefs. To not only dissolve and untwist cognitive distortions, but to also be, live, act as my highest self, 100% of the time.

Good luck in your transformation. Use your internal GPS system to help guide you. Do the next right thing, no matter the consequences. Until then, generate feelings of joyfulness, love, health and abundance. Always showing sincere appreciation and genuine Gratitude.

"It's what we don't say, that weighs the most." Unknown

No more limits,

Smiley

Made in the USA
Columbia, SC
28 July 2024